HIDDEN
ESSEX

CW00662817

HIDDEN
ESSEX

Stan Jarvis

With illustrations by Joan Bill

COUNTRYSIDE BOOKS
NEWBURY, BERKSHIRE

First Published 1989
Reprinted 1991
© Stan Jarvis 1989

COUNTRYSIDE BOOKS
3 Catherine Road
Newbury, Berkshire

ISBN 1 85306 048 8

Front Cover Photograph of Witham
taken by John Bethell

Produced through MRM Associates Ltd, Reading
Typeset by Acorn Bookwork, Salisbury
Printed in England by J. W. Arrowsmith Ltd, Bristol

Introduction

➤ Twenty-five years as a librarian in the county town, with its excellent collection of books on local history, turned me from a Hampshire Hog into an Essex Calf. Walking, cycling and motoring round the county brought me to an appreciation of Essex which I wanted to share with other people. The hesitant offering of my first book in 1968 was met with such encouragement that I found my 'metier' in the delving into the original documents in the Essex Record Office, the libraries, solicitors' offices, newspapers and private files, then seeing the places to which those documents referred as they appear today, and so producing books for modern people – books that interpret the past without the readers requiring knowledge of early kinds of handwriting or of Latin.

I was extremely fortunate in meeting Nicholas Battle at the point when he was considering the publishing of a book on smuggling in East Anglia. We found we worked very well together, so when he proposed a book on 'hidden Essex' I was delighted to undertake the research and writing. The difficulty has been the selection necessary from the abundance of fact and fancy concerning places and people not usually found in the standard guide books. The idea is that after reading this book a visit to a particular place will be enhanced through the knowledge of some happening which can add a new dimension to one's appreciation.

Access to places like churches, houses and gardens, libraries and museums is best checked with the tourist information service at county hall or at selected points in the county as shown in telephone directories. No author should claim to be infallible. Time changes buildings, alters stated facts week by week. If there are errors of fact in this book they are mine not the publisher's, and I shall be pleased to be informed of them for correction in future editions.

Stan Jarvis
1991

Abberton

The reservoir, completed in 1941, is capable of holding 6,000 million gallons of water within its twelve-mile circumference. The village of Abberton, which lies at its north east tip has gained more fame around the world as the home of this gigantic tank of water than ever it did in all its 2,000 years of existence as a settlement of man. The water does not gravitate there naturally, it is pumped directly from the river Stour north east of Colchester. It guarantees a six-month supply to the whole area of the Essex Water Company, whatever the weather.

Through sympathetic landscaping and tree planting the reservoir has, after 50 years, become such a natural feature that its true purpose can easily be overlooked by the tourist who would probably call it a lake. In fact, it was called the Colchester Lake, just after it was completed, by the Dam Busters of the Royal Air Force, led by Guy Gibson, V.C., because they used it in practice flights for the breaching of the Mohne and Eder dams on 16th May 1942, in a classic demonstration of pin-point bombing.

That incident may now be forgotten but the Abberton reservoir still has a world-wide reputation as a bird sanctuary. The ringing of birds had started here as early as 1949. By the time it was officially recognised as a sanctuary in 1967 more than 100,000 birds had been ringed and their subsequent arrivals recorded. Today, visitors are provided with opportunities to watch birds on the reservoir and its banks from a hide some 30 yards in length. The Essex Water Company takes its responsibilities in this area of the environment very seriously. It issues a free booklet summing up the value of this famous bird-watching centre:

'The Company hopes that the site will service the serious bird watcher and that it will also provide a centre to which families can come to see the wild birds and that it will encourage future generations of bird watchers and people interested in preservation of our wild life heritage.'

7

The wide variety of birds which use the reservoir like a service station on migration, or as a home right through the breeding season is not disturbed by the fishermen who find the place a paradise for a day's coarse fishing where a pike and a bream have been taken weighing 33 and ten and a half pounds respectively.

Aldham

Aldham is such a pretty place, and the villagers are very much alive to the fact. They get together on a Sunday in June to open some 20 of their gardens to the public, from Hall to modest semi. But Aldham was already well-known for a much older, historical, association. For years a certain tombstone stood in the old churchyard, which, when the new church was built a mile away in 1855, reverted to a wilderness. The old church was demolished, all except the ancient south porch which was integrated in the fabric of the new church. The tombstones in the old churchyard mouldered away for a hundred years. Then the rector was able to obtain permission to close the graveyard officially and to remove those stones still standing to the present churchyard.

One of those stones commemorated the burial of a certain Philip Morant who had been the rector here from 1745. He held the living still in 1767 when his wife died and he went to London to live with his daughter. On his death in 1770 his body was brought to Aldham for burial in the parish where he had found much happiness. His tombstone survived, so when the transfer was made from old to new, Philip Morant's memorial was not left in the churchyard but taken into the church itself to act as a special monument to a man who was not just a former rector but a man who had become famous as the first person ever to have written, printed and published a complete history of the county of Essex.

Philip Morant was born in Jersey in 1700 and educated in England. From university here he obtained a curacy at Great Waltham where the vicar was the erudite historian Dr Nicholas Tindal. From him Morant learned much of the technique of historical research and presentation, as well as being able to acquire some of his collections of original documents and transcripts. Morant moved on to various livings in Essex as a fully-fledged clergyman. He married Anne Stebbing, a rich heiress of Great Tey when he was 39 and settled at last in Aldham in 1745.

Here he tackled the awesome task of writing his *History and Antiquities of the County of Essex* which, supported by advance subscription, appeared in parts through eight years from 1760. The influence of this great work is evident in every history produced since then. Yet on his death Philip Morant's memorial was a simple tombstone inscribed:

BENEATH THIS STONE
ARE DEPOSITED THE REMAINS OF
THE REVD. PHILIP MORANT, A. M.,
25 YEARS RECTOR of this Parish,
died November 25th 1770.
Aged 70.
Also of Anne his Wife,
died July 28th 1767
Aged 69.

One section of Essex people was concerned that, after the removal of the tombstone from the old graveyard to the new it would erode away to illegibility and this last reminder of our own historian would be lost to future generations. So they paid for its restoration and its setting up inside the church, with a plaque beside it explaining:

The Reverend
PHILIP MORANT
M.A., F.S.A., Essex Historian
Rector of Aldham 1745–1770
This stone brought from his
burial place in the old churchyard
was restored and placed here by
The Essex Archaeological Society
A.D. 1966

When we leave the church by the timber-framed 14th century south porch we can sense his presence, his strong personality and we resolve to look up those two big volumes of his next time we are in the library.

Alresford

➤ There is a place in Hampshire called Alresford – famous for its watercress; and here in Essex there is another Alresford noted for its Roman villa. The watercress can still be seen in any good greengrocer's, but the villa has long since been hidden by a modern house built on top of it. Why should two such different places have the same name? The experts are stumped. As far as Essex goes they suggest that Aegel was a Saxon who owned the land where the traveller along the track from Wivenhoe to Brightlingsea could most safely ford the Alresford creek, the outflow of the Frating brook.

The Romans must have ridden this way many a time as commuters to Colchester in the first century when it was the premier town in England, far-flung outpost of the Roman empire. The villa was built very handily for just such a commuter, on a site very close to the present Alresford Lodge, where Alresford creek empties into the river Colne; a beautiful place to build a desirable residence with views all down the estuary on the one hand and gently rolling woodland on the other.

It is over a century ago that C. Golding and his archaeological friends, with the permission of farmer M. H. Barton, uncovered a corridor with a tessellated floor more than 100 yards long and a room with a central, decorated floor panel some 20 ft square. Further evidence that it was Roman was found in the flue tiles of the cunningly arranged central heating system via hypocausts. The Victoria County History sums up the situation today: 'A modern house now covers the villa site and the Roman pavements have been torn up and partly relaid.'

Where once the Roman officer drove his chariot to the garrison at Colchester the modern warrior of business rushes by electric train right through Colchester and on to London. Estates have quickly grown at Alresford to make come true the business man's dream of living in the country whilst working in the capital.

Althorne

➤ Go to Althorne station and you step back at least 50 years. The seats on the little platform beside the single line still have cast iron legs which form the monogram GER – Great Eastern Railway. That means they are coming up to 100 years old! The Crouch Valley Line, from Wickford to Southminster is under threat of closure because it is not used enough, yet there have been settlers here since the 6th century when the Saxons, coming up the Crouch in their boats, saw that this would be a good place to stay if they burned off all the prickly underbrush. That is why they gave it the name of Althorne, meaning, in their language, 'burnt thorn bush'.

But where was the centre of their settlement? It is a place which has developed several nuclei of village togetherness. That station platform sees a daily club of commuters depart and arrive. Their gossip brings the place to life for a moment, then its sinks into slumber till the evening homecoming once again reminds one of the bustle this branch line saw when it was opened, in the days before the car was king and everyone and everything went down the line to London. 'Use it or lose it' posed a question mark over its future when we stood on the platform in the spring sunshine. One lone daffodil dancing in the breeze showed how once the station gardens were so proudly and perfectly kept.

The oldest place of gathering and gossiping must be the church, now not much more patronised than the railway. Its ancient font, strangely carved, and its modern chancel show how the building, and the belief it represents, has seen times of crisis worse than the present materialistic indifference. A brass to William Hyklott, dated 1508, declares that he 'paide for the werkemanship of the wall of this churche'. If you go there say a prayer for William and a crowd of people like him

11

who, through 1,000 years, have preserved this place of peace for us to appreciate today.

Another place of assembly and social intercourse is the Black Lion where, behind the 18th century clapboard walls there is company, congenial, restful or boisterous as you please – a connection with the old Althorne reflected in the wooden cottages which gather round. How is it then that the villagers chose such an isolated site for their memorial to the village heroes of the First World War, to which the later names were added? It stands on a triangle of rough grass at the junction where Station Road runs down from Burnham Road. The point is this: the villagers did not just pay for the memorial, they got together, came to this place, and with their own hands built this structure of massive oak beams under a tiled roof simply to protect from the elements the list of names of those who went away and did not come back.

Ashdon

➤ 'The church forms a picturesque object on the hilltop as one approaches from Radwinter' says my tattered, century-old guidebook. That church of All Saints shows in its windows and its walls an ancestry going back 600 years. The history it has made, the life and death it has celebrated throughout all that time would be an amazement in any other parish, but here it must be set beside the ancient burial mounds, the Bartlow Hills, which were raised nearly 2,000 years ago; at the same time, it is thought, as the villa on Great Copt Hill was being built by those upstart invaders, the Romans.

The ancient British people would smile to know that the villa is now just a scatter of unidentifiable rubble in a field while their great mounds of earth can still be seen. That is to say **some** of them have survived. At 45 ft high and around 140 ft in circumference at the base, their destruction by levelling was not so easy, but after all those years some have disappeared, so that of the original eight only four are left. One hill was dug away completely in 1586 so that the land could be brought into cultivation. In 1832 three more were flattened for the same purpose, on the order of the land-owner Henry, Viscount Maynard. Since he was a man sensitive to the historical value of these mounds he made sure they were taken apart carefully. He was rewarded with the discovery of glass bottles holding the ashes of human cremation 2,000 years ago, along with the various utensils which would have been used as a burial ritual.

All these valuable reminders of the life here of some great British family which had to make its peace with the Romans were kept at Lord Maynard's home, Easton Lodge, at Little Easton. Sad to say the house was burned down in 1847 and all those items were destroyed. Accurate descriptions had, fortunately, been put on record and there are still some objects from the other mounds kept in the Saffron Walden Museum.

Ashdon can boast of famous Britons in modern times. One is the author Spike Mays who, in books like *Reuben's Corner*, and *Five Miles from Bunkum* (in association with Christopher Ketteridge) paints a fascinating picture of the last, lingering self-sufficient days of this beautiful village when he grew up here from 1914. The *Haverhill Echo* says, in his *Return to Anglia* that he has been a customer at the Ashdon Bonnett since that date, but since that would make him about seven years old we should, perhaps, take Spike's first pint with a pinch of salt. It is with a salty wit that Spike looks at life in the Ashdon of his day, then compares it with what he saw on a visit in the 1980s. The look of the place is summed up: 'Where once was wilderness throbbing with life in tangles of overgrown hedgerows, profusions of wild flowers and wonderful birdsong from finch, tit, warbler, linnet and lark, the croak of the moorhen and rainbow flashes from kingfishers, there are "improvements". Tidiness prevails, neatness abounds and the village has won awards for The Best Kept Village.'

That village has also been seen through the eyes of another famous person, Robert Gibson, Master of Rutherford College, Public Orator at the University of Kent and authority on French literature. He came to Ashdon as a London schoolboy, to help with the harvest in 1944 when the village men were away at the war. He fell in love with it, through the years researched its history, and produced his book *Annals of Ashdon: no ordinary village* which was published by the Essex Record Office in 1988. It can be truly said that he has revealed the hidden history of Ashdon.

Asheldham

➤ As gold was to Kimberley so gravel was to Asheldham. It was mined by rolling back a blanket of earth which was folded back again as the great drag-lines moved on to the next site. Before all was swept away archaeologists were able to find evidence that here, flat as the countryside is, a hill fort was established in prehistoric times something less than half a mile from the church of St. Lawrence. A plateau was formed after clearing the forest on which there settled an Ancient British tribe. That was 1,000 years and more before the Saxons came on the scene, and between the two the Romans left evidence of their presence from the second half of the first century.

On this plateau the settlers, or their successors heaped up an oval rampart enclosing 16 acres. From it, in recent years, Bronze Age, Iron Age and Saxon detritus has been recovered. Inside this ring the Saxon village with Hall and church grew up. It has been suggested, as a result of further excavation, that the first church was all of timber, replaced in the 14th century with a building of rubble stone, incorporating Roman brick. The strong, squat tower now sports brick battlements of much later date.

The intriguing feature of this church is not in its architecture but in its use today. After eight years of sorry deterioration it was declared redundant in 1986, but then it took on a new job which has made it busier than it was for years as a parish church. The Diocesan Youth Centre was looking for a building where young people could stay weekends and enjoy their first experience in adventure and activity with a bunch of friends in the countryside. This church was a splendid location and, with an upper storey introduced, it was just the right size to accommodate up to 38 people, including group leaders, with a kitchen and a games room also provided. Groups organised by the social services and probation officers have enjoyed the sailing, walking, bird-watching, painting, drawing and other activities out in the air and back in the church, where the young people look after themselves in cooking and housekeeping.

St. Lawrence's, revitalised by volunteers' hard work, has a place in a community far wider than its builders could ever have contemplated.

Ashingdon

➤ Where was the Battle of Assandune fought? It was the fight between the armies of Canute and Edmund Ironside on 18th October 1016. Canute, the Dane, had led his men on a ravaging expedition through Kent, with the subjugation of Mercia his ultimate aim. The English, under Edmund, could not catch up with the Danes, let alone bring them to battle, until they were on their way back through Essex. Here – was it at Ashdon or Ashingdon? – Edmund at last came up with them. Battle was joined and the Danes were triumphant. Some people say the English were betrayed by one of their own men.

'Assandune' is identified enthusiastically by P. H. Reaney, the place-name expert, as Ashingdon, though people in the past had favoured Ashdon. The former is in the south of the county below the river Crouch and adjoining Canewdon while Ashdon is far to the north on the very border of the county, running down to the bank of the Stour. Herbert Tompkins, writing in 1938 is adamant: 'There are, we know, still doubting Thomases who suggest the possibility that the fight was at Ashdon near Saffron Walden, or at one of the other Ashingdons or Ashendons in England; we need not heed them.'

It has been proposed that Canute had camped on Canewdon Hill and people have been tempted to find a relationship between the two names, but Canewdon had been named as the settlement of 'Cana's people' long before the Danes arrived on the scene. Edmund Ironside had halted his men on the neighbouring Ashingdon Hill. The battlefield was the plain between them. Let Charles Dickens, no less, tell us the outcome: '. . . then Ironside, who was a big man, proposed to Canute, who was a little man, that they two should fight it out in single combat. If Canute had been a big man, he would probably have said yes, but being the little man, he decidedly said no. However, he declared that he was willing to divide the kingdom – to take all that lay north of Watling Street, as the old Roman military road from Dover to Chester was called, and to give Ironside all that lay south of it. Most men being weary of so much bloodshed, this was done. But Canute soon became sole King of England; for Ironside died suddenly within two months. Some think he was killed, and killed by Canute's orders. No one knows.'

The present church of St. Andrew has a nave and a chancel which have been dated to the 14th century but even that is not old enough for us to be able to say that the English and the Danes would have seen it. But it was on this very site, some four years after his victory, that the new King Canute ordered a church to be built as a celebration of this great turning point in his life. There is not much doubt that the Roman bricks purloined by his builders were incorporated in the later church.

We must lift up our eyes to see the unusual modern feature of St. Andrew's – the clock which commemorates the coronation of King Edward the Seventh. Instead of the numbers of the hours we see the letters of the King's name, EDWARDUS VII REX, starting at 11 o'clock. At the top the Royal Arms are emblazoned and at the bottom there is shown the date of Edward's death 'AD MCMX' – 1910.

Aythorpe Roding

➤ A windmill of white weatherboarding throwing its white sails like arms to the blue sky above the brown thatch of the cottage before it, with the green of the trees rustling in the breeze as a backdrop. A nostalgic dream you might say, but no, it is a practical reality here in one of the parishes taking part of their names from the Roding stream, growing bigger and bolder on its way down to Barking creek.

16

Aythorpe Roding postmill

The mill is a postmill, of the type which, built round a central post, is bodily turned round to face the wind. Beneath the mill is the 'roundhouse' protecting that central post and acting as the miller's storeroom and workspace. Taken into the care of the County Council, this mill was completely restored by 1982. Proof of the thoroughness of that restoration is shown in the fact that on completion on 3rd March it was brought into the wind, the sails turned smoothly and about two hundredweight of wheat was soon ground into flour. It was originally built in 1779, when the land on which it stands belonged to Sir Fitzwilliam Barrington. In those days the roundhouse was no more than an open shed. The last working miller was Jack Belsham, remembered affectionately by older inhabitants, truly a jolly miller. That was well before the last war. By 1936 the sails were so rotten that it was no longer safe to chance them in the wind.

From the 15th century in the belfry beneath the broached spire of the church of the Virgin Mary the three bells have pealed:

'Those ancient bells in the steeple
A million times have rung.
Their message is clear, I am here, I am here,
Won't you come, won't you come, won't you come?'

The man who wrote these lines was a local farmer and churchwarden for 30 years, Victor Gunn. He was born in Buckhurst Hill where his father was gardener to the Pelly family, and an independent man of business acumen. When sacked for his outspokenness he rented a farm at Margaret Roding and by the end of the First World War was well established not only as a farmer but also as a transport contractor. Vic, one of six children, left school when he was 14 and went straight into the family business doing hard labour on the farm until he was old enough to learn to drive and so help on the transport side of the business. He married his childhood sweetheart when he was 26, in 1933. The family business was doing so well on the transport side that they were able to rent Cut Elms Farm in Aythorpe Roding as well as White Roding mill.

During the Second World War Vic was his father's right-hand man, getting through an enormous amount of work in carrying goods of all kinds which were vital to the locality when fuel was rationed and supplies hard to come by. Life was difficult, times were hard – Vic turned to poetry for his relief; not reading it but writing it, under the benign influence of Jack Shearman of nearby Peppers Green.

With the end of the war and the nationalisation of road transport Vic was able to see his father into retirement and, for his own family, buy Cut Elms Farm. Now he had long days on the tractor preparing the ground and harvesting the crops, and so he had the time to ponder on his poetry, to carry it in his head through the long day and write it down of an evening whilst other men would be watching television or hailing their friends in the pub or the club. Vic died in 1978. No plaque records his dwelling here, but there is a wonderful memorial to him. It is the slim paperback in which he had published eleven of his own, favourite poems back in 1972. There is a copy in the Chelmsford library.

Barling

➤ Look at the map and see where Barling stands. Due south is Shoeburyness and the extremity of the Thames estuary. To the east the marshes spread where creeks and dikes made a watery cobweb round the islands of Potton, Rushley, Havengore and New England. Northwards the Barling Marsh runs to the bank of the Roach. Only westward is there a connection with the wider world. The age of the car has brought Barling into focus as a very desirable place in which to live in secluded peace. But if more houses are built the ancient form and personality of the village will be destroyed. Old inhabitants have taken exception to the recent additions – the kind of estate houses which have been set down in villages all over the country. One night in 1988 a newly built house was set on fire by an arsonist. The culprit has not been found. Was it a last, despairing protest at the blatant, brash invasion of this peaceful place?

There was a time when Barling was bigger – and split into Great and Little. The Little was so small it got lost and it is only from the air that cropmarks show where its church once stood – to the north west in the region of Bolts Farm. When it was calling people to prayer there was a quay on the river bank where boats and barges could unload. Those busy days are now well behind it.

The south wall of the parish church of All Saints proves that it was built in Norman times. The land here was owned by the King himself. It was Edward the Confessor (1042–1066) who ceded it to St. Paul's cathedral. That is why some local records were lost in the Great Fire of London in 1666. There is an unusual monument which makes a visit to the church worthwhile. It is a model of the windmill which stood about 200 yards north west of the church from 1763 until 1946. The trouble was that it started listing badly in 1903, and with the advent of steam engines the obsolete windmill was just not worth repairing. The sails were lowered to the ground in 1907 then the mill mouldered away to its eventual demolition. The model was made by Harry Manning, descendant of the last miller, Frederick Manning. He made it when he was 82. After his death his widow presented it to the church for display in his memory. It was a very pleasant thought, for the mill and the church were what we might call the skyscrapers of the village, looking out over it together through two centuries.

Battlesbridge

➤ Battlesbridge is not a village in itself, it is a hamlet of Rettendon. Even as late as 1937 the directory was showing it as two separate words. One reason for its development was its situation on the bank of the Crouch and the use of that river for transport from the earliest times. Later, a station was built here, on the Maldon and Southminster branch of what was then the London and North Eastern Railway, to take on that role of goods transport and to serve the people of Rettendon and its hinterland. The directory also shows that the Matthews, well-known as milling and cattle and dog food manufacturers were living at the mill house and that the mill, one of ten they owned, was in full production. Another name of note was Meeson, for William Taylor Meeson was the miller before Matthews took over.

The interesting point about the old, water-driven mill that stood astride the creek is that it was not a river mill. The Crouch flows so slowly that it does not have the strength to turn a wheel, but there is a strong tidal flow well past Battlesbridge. So some clever fellow, whose name is lost in the mists of history, built a tidal mill – the only mill ever to work on the Crouch. It must have required many men and much effort to dam the creek with an embankment and to build a rough, wooden mill upon it. Time brought improvement and development. By 1775 it had been rebuilt with four floors and four pairs of stones, grinding wheat into flour as fast as the barges could unload it.

It would have been burned down in 1815 but for the quickness of a workman who slammed a door to stop the draught and disengaged the stones. The flame of a candle caused a 'flash-over' in the dusty atmosphere, but that brave man prevented its spread. The Meesons came with new ideas for new times. They demolished the old tide mill around 1902 and turned over to steam in a new mill on the seaward side of the bridge which takes the road across the creek. The only reminder now left of that old mill is the remnant of brickwork on the bank which formed the dam, and a piece of broken wall of the mill itself.

Battlesbridge has been bypassed, so it is now a pleasantly quiet place to visit, and very worthwhile, not just for its scenery and its two old pubs, the Harp and the Barge, but also for the large collection of antiques and 'bygones' shops which have congregated here. One can stand by the river and muse that the Crouch had been a regular route for smugglers from the 18th century. They were still creeping up the Crouch as late as 1833 when the brig *Mary*, searched here at Battlesbridge, was found to have a vast quantity of tobacco and brandy worth £3,000 in the money of the day, hidden deep under its legitimate cargo of coal.

By the way, there was no battle fought out here to give the bridge its name. It is thought that Battlesbridge originated from the fact that the Battaile family were the local land-owners from as early as 1300.

Beaumont-cum-Moze

Beaumont Quay has crumbled away. Two hundred years ago it was busy by day and by night. During the day there was a procession of small boats and barges wending its way through the marshy maze from Hamford Water to the quay with coal from Newcastle and luxuries from London for the farmers and their families in north east Essex. At night with muffled oars the smugglers stealthily rowed in with all kinds of contraband brought across the Channel in their swift-sailing sloops. With carts and horses waiting on the wharf, smuggled goods from gin to jewellery and from tea to tapestry could be in Ipswich or in London as the new day dawned.

There were few people to become curious about these dark night doings; the quay was miles away from the village of Beaumont, and that was a place so small that in 1678 it was united with the even smaller parish of Moze, so that the parishioners of both could pull down the dilapidated church at Moze and carry the stone and timber over to Beaumont to repair St Leonard's church there and make it safe and sound for worship through another 100 years. Once again it suffered from the ravages of time and weather and so, in 1854, it was again rebuilt, to the design of architect C. Hakewill who retained some of the old fabric.

This means it is not now as old as Beaumont Hall, a wonderful example of 17th century Essex expertise in brickwork tucked away down its drive off the A136. And this remarkable building replaced a much earlier house on this site. Moze means 'marshy land' in the language of the Saxon settlers. Even before their presence here some Ancient British tribe had solved the problem of obtaining salt from the sea. The Domesday Book shows that way out on the marshes they had dug out salt pans, three at Moze and two at Beaumont where, when the heat of the sun was insufficient, they boiled seawater in wide pans over huge bonfires and scraped up the salty sediment. In trade then it was as good as gold.

The attractions for the traveller today include the wide views across wide fields to the marshes and the famous fishermen's seamark – the tower on the Naze.

Beeleigh

➤ Beeleigh is not a village; it is part of the parish of St. Peter, Maldon. But there was a time when it was a separate little settlement carved out of the primeval forest where bees had been so numerous and troublesome that the Saxon fellers called it the 'bee' clearing. It was not long, historically speaking, before it was absorbed into Maldon for the purposes of parish government.

The building which still brings significance to the name is Beeleigh Abbey, built in 1180 to house an outlier of the Premonstratensian house of White Canons at Great Parndon. The man who led them here, Robert Mantell, is shown as one of the figures of celebrated Maldon people decorating the south wall of All Saints church in Maldon. For over 350 years this small abbey flourished. The brothers farmed the fields and carried the corn to the watermill they built on the riverbank.

Then came the Dissolution of the Monasteries; the abbey was granted to John Gate, Esquire, in 1540 and nine years later he sold it to William Marche who had an extension built on to increase the living accommodation. It must have looked raw and brash at the time, but now its brick-filled timber framing so merges with the rubble stone of the abbey that the difference in age is quite forgotten. From the iron gates the appearance of these tall old buildings in a sylvan setting is a photographer's dream. It has to remain a dream for the house and grounds are strictly private. In those days of alteration and repair stone coffins holding human remains were dug up under the ruins of the abbey buildings, and there has been a whisper of hidden treasure being found.

From here there is a beautiful walk past Beeleigh Grange, where the painter Sir Edwin Landseer spent many a holiday, to the meeting of the waters. The Chelmer, the Blackwater and the canal are crossed by numerous bridges as the footpath wends its way through a copse to cross the footbridge over the falls – a grand sight when the river is in flood. One of those bridges, over the canal as it strikes straight for Heybridge Basin alongside the Maldon golf course, was built by the canal 'Navvies' around 1790.

Berden

➤ Isolated from the arteries of traffic, bordering Hertfordshire six miles north west of Stansted Mountfitchet, Berden still offers a comparatively calm environment, evocative of the days when the horse ruled the road and pulled the plough. Far back in those days the buildings of a little priory were erected for a small band of Augustinian monks, half a mile north of the present church, on the bank of a tributary of the river Stort. It seems common knowledge that this priory was here, yet there is neither stick nor stone left on the site today to prove its presence.

That is one enigma. The second is that a copper bracelet found in a Bronze Age burial in Berden has been lost. No-one knows who has it now. It was back in 1907 when the foundations for a new Wesleyan chapel were being dug, on the site of the present village hall, that a workman put his pick through a skull and flourished it aloft. He prised it off and left it in the trench with other bones while he had his lunch. When he returned the skull and some of the bones had been taken. An earthenware pot and the rest of the bones eventually found their way to the Saffron Walden Museum. That interesting copper bracelet was sold by the builder to a Saffron Walden dealer, but further enquiries as to who then acquired it were met with stony silence. The people who did care about this remarkable evidence of an ancient settlement here eventually got to hear of the circumstances, but they had to wait until those village labourers returned safely from the First World War to establish the archaeological details. All the rubble from that excavation was disposed of by dropping it down an old well in the grounds of Berden Hall. That will surely confuse the archaeologists of the future.

The third enigma confronts us on Stock's Farm south of the church. It is a man-made mound some ten ft high and 120 ft around its base. It is said to be the motte of a motte and bailey castle. It is true that the remains of a moat still wash its foot, but who built it in this beautiful backwater of Essex? Why – and when? Even the expert, Pevsner, can only say, 'The origin is uncertain'.

On the site of the priory, The Priory was built, a beautiful Tudor house with that characteristic warm, red brick and exposed timberwork. A building in what was once the farmyard is a 17th century well-house erected over a well so deep that extra power was needed to bring the bucket up. That power was provided by a great wheel, a treadmill inside which a servant trod wearily until the cisterns in the house were once more filled to the brim.

As to the church, let us quote a local historian, 'We have no ornate tombs or wonderful stained glass, just a gem of a small country church dedicated to St Nicholas.'

Berechurch

➤ Due south of Colchester's town centre and now part of that borough is the village of Berechurch, formerly known as West Donyland. In that name it recalls Dunna, the Saxon chief who brought his tribe to settle in this favoured spot which travellers came to know as Dunna's Land. Through the centuries the place grew and separated into East and West entities. The western enclave soon took the name of Berechurch, an Anglo-Saxon appellation for a church with a wooden tower, timber-framed and weatherboarded, a landmark and a ready identification for wayfarers. That church, of St. Michael, is still worth a visit, dating as it does largely from the beginning of the 16th century. Within it many of the Awdeleys, or Audleys, were laid to rest. The connection of this family with Essex goes right back to the 15th century when a clever young boy born to working class parents climbed the ladder of ambition to the point where he became the Lord Chancellor of England – and Lord Audley of Walden.

He had become Town Clerk of Colchester when he was only 28 and was a Member of Parliament at 35. Six years later he was Speaker of the House of Commons, had the ear of the King and was well on the way to fame and fortune of which his parents could never have dreamed. In the process he had to stoop to some mean acts in supporting Henry VIII's divorces, but his conscience was stilled by the large tracts of land and the many buildings given him by the King who had confiscated them at the Dissolution of the Monasteries. They included Walden Abbey – hence his peerage in that name. But he was not forgotten or forgiven by some people. When he died in 1544 and was buried under a grand monument in Saffron Walden church, Fuller, in his *Worthies* . . . said of it, '. . . the marble was not blacker than the soul, nor harder than the heart, of him whose bones were laid beneath it . . .'.

He had no sons, but the Audleys' connection with Essex was continued by his brother to whom he left the manor of Berechurch. His descendants enjoyed Berechurch and the fruits of its lands, the money from its rents, for nearly 300 years. Then Henry Audley, last of the line, weak, foolish, totally self-indulgent, ran through all that inheritance, left his wife, and ended up in the Fleet Prison, owing thousands to an army of creditors. It was his widow who, on being told of his death, put up the money for his body to be collected from the Fleet and taken to Berechurch for burial amongst his kith and kin.

Berners Roding

The Roding is the river which waters, and gives its name to eight villages. Berners was the family which ruled here in the days when William the Conqueror handed out his favours. The Domesday Book of 1086 shows Hugh de Berners living here at the Hall. As we know from our history books the road through life for courtiers and politicians was rich but risky. Hugh's descendant Sir James Berners was still enjoying his inheritance 300 years later when he threw in his lot with Richard II. He backed the wrong horse, when Richard was deposed Sir James was executed.

One person who mourned his untimely death was his daughter Dame Juliana Berners. She had been a loved and well brought up daughter, born here in the country with the wide-spreading forest of Essex right on her doorstep. Little wonder, then, that she could ride and hunt and hold a hawk with the best of the lords and ladies who shone with excitement in the company of the King. She seemed to enjoy all the sports which should have been the preserve of the young lords and their squires.

As she came of age she threw off those excesses of youth and was appointed the Prioress of Sopwell Nunnery, in those days a place renowned for the education of the elite. Here she had the time and the peaceful atmosphere in which to write. But her writings were not sacred – they were all about the very subjects which she knew so thoroughly from her youthful experience, riding, hawking, hunting. Since this was 100 years before the invention of printing she had to write it all in her own fair hand and set her nuns to copy it for further circulation. When Wynkyn de Worde set up his printing press on Caxton's death in 1491 one of the first books he produced was the *Treatyse Perteynynge to Hawkynge, Huntynge, Fyshynge, and Coot Armiris* – and it was Juliana's manuscript which formed its basis.

Today the hamlet of Berners Roding is down a tiny lane which ends in a cart track, largely forgotten by the increasingly noisy world. The church is so old that its dedication has been forgotten. Juliana would have walked beside its thick old walls, but her Hall has long since been rebuilt. This is a splendidly isolated place, with opportunities for walks along footpaths and bridleways.

Billericay

When, in 1988, the County Council invited folk to submit names of people and places suitable for commemoration by plaques during Essex Heritage Year the general desire in Billericay was to mark the Chantry House, now an Indian restaurant, as the home of Christopher Martin, the 'treasurer' of the Pilgrim Fathers who made that great death-defying journey to the New World in 1620. Christopher was a miller who married Mary Prower in the parish church of Great Burstead, of which Billericay was then but a hamlet.

He was a man of an independent turn of mind in a group of people who were determined to pursue their religious beliefs and practices despite official prohibition. When persecution by the established church became unbearable they moved as a group to Holland, from where Martin and two friends came back to look for a ship which could take them all the way across the Atlantic – the ship they recommended was the *Mayflower*.

They sailed it round to Leigh, here in Essex, took on their stores and set off round the coast of southern England in the summer of 1620, making Plymouth their last port of call. Even then they were already a long way from the Chantry House, but what a voyage lay before them! Christopher Martin, Mary his wife and her brother Solomon Prower all survived to reach the Massachusetts coast, but sadly they all died that winter during the hard life on the ship whilst they were building the colony ashore.

The proof that Christopher Martin actually lived in the Chantry House was too tenuous to satisfy the Heritage plaque scheme so a substitute was suggested. There was another person whose residence in Billericay could be well proved, though his claim to fame was not on the same spiritual level – much more to do with the flesh. Thomas Wood was known as 'the ghastly miller'. First he was famous for his fatness, then for his determination in dieting. He lived in the recently restored mill house on Bell Hill now known as Mill House, and looked after a pair of mills which once stood nearby, each side of the road to Wickford. One of these windmills was there in the 16th century and there is a local oral tradition that it ground the flour for that epic voyage of the Pilgrim Fathers. The other first appears on a map in 1777.

Thomas Wood was born in 1719 into a milling family. It is known that in adulthood he signed a 21 year lease of the mill from Lord Petre. He was a prosperous man, and showed it in his dress and in his figure. By the time he was 40 he weighed some 25 stone and was the butt of good-humoured banter, and was pointed out to travellers as a local landmark, with some pride. He took it all in good part, standing stoutly at the mill door with a kindly word for all.

But within three years his fatness quickly took toll of his fitness – he began to ache all over, from his head to his feet; he lost his voice, he lost his teeth and was close to losing heart. It was his friend John Powley, rector of neighbouring Nevendon who came to the rescue, giving him a book to read all about the healthfulness of the sober and moderate diet. Thomas got hooked on it. In a very short time he became teetotal, gave up eating meat, began using dumbbells for exercise and took a cold bath twice a week. It was reckoned that he had soon lost eleven stone in weight, but since he was too superstitious to sit on one of those new-fangled weighing machines the exact weight could not be verified. He was, in his own words, 'gradually transformed from a monster to a person of moderate size'.

From July 1767 he ate no food other than a kind of dumpling made every day from one pound of flour boiled in

The Chantry House, Billericay

one and a half pints of milk. When he had to spend the day at Romford market he took the ingredients along with him and had them boiled up at the inn. The story of his success was spread world-wide, encouraging people to write to him for his advice in all kinds of medical problems. He answered them all with patience and understanding. The trouble was that very few people were able to match his amazing determination in sticking to such a rigid diet. It certainly was effective for he lived to the good old age, for those days, of 63 and lies with ancestors and descendants in Burstead churchyard.

Birdbrook

Martha Blewit as a name seems rather ordinary, yet it has a particular claim to fame, and has been remembered now for more than 300 years. Martha was the wife of the landlord of the Swan Inn and lived an uneventful life in the village, dying in 1681. She did something which very few people have done in all the years since her death – she married no less than nine husbands, to be outlived by the last. A tablet in the church tower reminds us of this fact. At her burial the priest chose as his text for the sermon, 'Last of all the woman died also'. Strangely enough there is another tablet in that same tower to the memory of Robert Hogan – who had seven wives!

As to the look of the place, there is an interesting passage in David Coller's history of Essex published in 1861; 'Of Birdbrook, which adjoins Steeple Bumpsted to the east, it was said in the last century – "In the passage from Toppesfield to this place, you are presented for upwards of half a mile with one of the finest landscapes in the county; but the pleasure received from this delightful prospect is in some measure damped upon your approach to the village, which has all the appearance of wretchedness and poverty; and indeed it is a matter of astonishment that a place so very inviting from its situation should be without one good house in it." This is a libel upon the Birdbrook of the present day. It has several neat mansions and good farm-houses; and Baythorne park, the property of Mr King Viall, standing on the acclivity above the Stour, with its park-like pastures and its fine old trees, is sufficient in itself to redeem the parish from the reproach of the surly traveller.'

The poverty of the periods of agricultural depression has gone, more professional people than ploughmen keep the houses in picturesque good order. As the writer of our day says in the district guide, '. . . as delightful a village as one could find in many a long day'.

Blackmore

➤ Such goings on at Blackmore! Such parties and performances, all at the royal behest. It was, after all, such a convenient place for Henry VIII to let his hair down; only 25 miles from London, yet buried in the country, where innocent pleasures could be enjoyed away from the gaze of gossips and the criticism of killjoys. Philip Morant, the 18th century historian of Essex says that Henry, '. . . when he had a mind to be lost with his courtesans often frequented the Priory . . .' at Blackmore. It is obvious that he was doing this before the dissolution of that priory in 1525, for it was here, in 1519, that Elizabeth Blount, one of the ladies in the retinue of Catherine of Aragon, was delivered of a son. Henry acknowledged him as his son and spoiled him thoroughly. When the boy was 14 he was engaged to the only daughter of the Duke of Norfolk, but by the time he was 17 he was dead. Now some people say that he was poisoned by Anne Boleyn and her brother, but who is to know today?

Henry liked Blackmore so much that he went there often, and told his courtiers he was not to be disturbed. Since the house of the former Priory of St Lawrence was known as Jericho House enquirers were told quite simply that the King had gone to Jericho – and that phrase is now part of our language. Not many villages can claim such a distinction! And that is why the little stream that fed the moat which surrounded all the priory buildings was nicknamed the Jordan.

The church we see today was the priors' chapel, but it lost its chancel when it was demolished after closure of the priory. Its greatest beauty, its finest feature, is the 15th century bell tower constructed entirely of huge wooden beams with timber cladding on a rubble foundation wall. Nikolaus Pevsner, the expert on buildings, goes into raptures over it, claiming it to be '. . . one of the most impressive, if not the most impressive, of all timber towers of England'. Even the local pub, the Bull Inn can boast that it is, in essence, nearly 500 years old. It does not see the grand life that it did when bluff King Hal filled it with his lords and ladies for a riotous weekend.

Black Notley

➤ It is just 60 years ago that the foundation stones of the hospital at Black Notley were laid. It was built at a cost of £78,000 to serve as a sanatorium for the care and the cure, if possible, of people afflicted with tuberculosis. Improved standards of living helped to drive away that dreaded disease and the hospital was made available under the National Health Service to general medical and nursing services. Now the big new District Hospital, built from the core of another tuberculosis sanatorium at Broomfield, has taken over most of the services for an area which includes Black Notley, so the future of what local people consider their own 'cottage' hospital is hanging in the balance.

With the coming of this sanatorium one member of the parish council put forward the idea that the name of the village should be changed from Black Notley to Light Notley, as this new sanatorium was a 'palace of sunshine and light' in the village. Nothing came of that idea, though it did get reported in the *Essex Chronicle*, where the reporter thought that White Notley got the first part of its name from the stream called the Guith, and Black Notley was so cold and drear that it was christened 'Bleak', altered to 'Black' by the march of time.

Turn to the expert, P. H. Reaney, and we find that Black Notley was formerly called Great Notley and White Notley was its Little neighbour, also called Dengayne because the Engaine family were Lords of the Manor. The most likely reason for their differentiation by colour is that one church was made of light-coloured stone and rubble which looked very white when it was first built – at White Notley; and the other church was tarred to protect its wooden walls from the weather – and what could be blacker than tar? So Black Notley it became.

It is a small enough and somewhat scattered village even today, with modern development opposite the hospital, but it has sent at least three sons out into the wide world, to fame, to fortune, or at least to mention in the history books. Could anyone have imagined that young Bill Bedell, born here back in 1571 would grow up to be a bishop? Clever enough to go to university, he took holy orders and became chaplain to Sir Henry Wotton, who was himself secretary to the Earl of Essex. Bedell accompanied him to Spain, Italy and Ireland. Then, after a period as a parish priest at Bury St Edmunds he was appointed Provost of Trinity College, Dublin, and two years later, Bishop of the two sees of Kilmore and Ardagh. He refused one of them on the principle that he could only serve one see at a time – an unusual gesture in times of veniality. In the 1642 rebellion, when he was already over 70, he was thrown into prison, along with his family. It was only for three weeks, but the privation was such that it led to his death.

Richard Symonds was born in Black Notley in 1617 and took a very different course in life. He became a soldier, loyally serving Charles I as a member of his lifeguards, surviving all the important battles in the Civil War and dying at a ripe old age in the last decade of the century. He kept a notebook of points of interest in the places he visited from one battle to another and that journal is as much the reason for his fame today as his service so close to the king.

The man who really put Black Notley on the map was John Ray, born in 1627 to the wife of the village blacksmith. He was lucky enough to get a rudimentary education at Braintree Grammar School, then but a converted chapel in the parish church. This enabled him to go on to Trinity College, Cambridge. He was so intelligent that he was elected a Fellow and continued at the College for 18 years. The subject which occupied his intellect and his life was natural history. At that time knowledge of the subject was scanty, with fact and fiction all mixed up together. Ray set himself to put in order man's recording of his natural surroundings, especially the field of botany.

Scholars from all over the world sent specimens for his opinion and advice as he worked on his great book on the history of plants which was published in three volumes between 1686 and 1704, covering some 11,000 species. His system of classification was so good that it continued in use for over 200 years. He died in 1705 in his 78th year and was buried under a lavish monument in the churchyard, paid for by the Bishop of London.

Boreham

Boreham's history is remarkable. Here in this small village kings and queens have strolled about, great statesmen have set up home and families of national note have been buried in the church. Let us start at the beginning. A former vicar, William T. Smith, says that Roman bricks are incorporated in the church of St. Andrew, so there is a clue to life in Boreham some 2,000 years ago. The Saxons followed them to give the place its name, interpreted as meaning a settlement with a market. Its importance is substantiated by its division at that time into six separate manors, Old Hall, New Hall, Culverts, Walkefares, Brent Hall and Porters. The last named stood as the oldest house in the village until it was pulled down to make way for the bypass. Boreham gets three entries in the Domesday Book and New Hall went on to be acquired by Henry VIII from Sir Thomas Boleyn around 1518 which he had rebuilt as 'Beaulieu'. He was still married to Catherine of Aragon when he richly celebrated the great Feast of St. George here in 1524. The Hall passed out of royal ownership in 1573, but not before it had been lived in by Queen Mary before her accession and Queen Elizabeth, who had her coat of arms carved over the entrance door.

It was she who granted it to the Radcliffes, Earls of Sussex, whose grand monument is such a feature of the church. The Hall was sold by them to George Villiers, Duke of Buckingham, for £30,000 in 1620, yet, 30 years and one civil war later it went for just five shillings. Since Villiers was a Royalist, Parliament seized his estates and offered this fabulous place to Oliver Cromwell for that nominal sum. He exchanged it very soon after for Hampton Court.

John Evelyn, the famous diarist described New Hall in detail and was much taken with it. The Villiers family recovered New Hall at the Restoration and sold it to General Monck, Duke of Albermarle, the man who so diplomatically bridged the gap between Parliamentarian and Royalist to effect the return of the Stuarts to the throne. Upon Charles II's marriage in 1661 Monck had Nell Gwynn and other court favourites come here to act *The Merry Wives of Windsor* in the vast hall of this mansion. The last royal visitor to stay here is thought to have been James II, who came in May 1686.

The Hall then experienced all sorts of vicissitudes and neglect as well as part demolition. But in 1798 it was purchased for the present owners, a community of the Regular Canonesses of the Holy Sepulchre, who established a school here. Today its reputation extends far beyond the county boundary.

In all that grandeur at Boreham spare a thought for one little, old lady who lived in the meanest cottage at the poorest end of the village. When cattle died, children were sick, or the butter would not churn they put the blame on her, she was bewitching them. Finally she was taken to court for witchcraft, hanged and buried in unconsecrated ground. You can still read the entry of that burial in the Boreham parish register where it shows that in 1593 'Mother Haven suffered at Boreham for Witchcraft'.

Bowers Gifford

➤ Where Basildon gives way to Southend, just before the roundabout junction of the A13 with the A1301, one passes through Bowers Gifford. It joins imperceptibly with North Benfleet to the north, but it is still a lonely lane which runs south to the old centre of the village. Bowers Hall has in its grounds the remains of a moat which surrounded the old Hall where lived the chief of the band of settlers who gave this place the name of Bowers – meaning quite simply a collection of cottages. In the 13th century the Giffards, or Giffords were holding this manor by service to the mighty Hugh Bigod, Earl of Norfolk. The Giffords were related quite closely to William the Conqueror on the distaff side, so Bowers Gifford was not an unimportant place.

That knightly connection is demonstrated in the church of St Margaret, now right on the edge of the railway. So lonely, though, that it has to be kept locked. In the chancel there is a large brass, probably life-size, which was made in about 1348 to mark the grave of Sir John Gifford. It is one of the oldest of military brasses, the third oldest in the county, and it is the last brass to show armour of complete mail. Regrettably the head, part of the right leg, part of the sword and the inscription are missing. His feet are shown resting on what appears to be an amicable-looking lion.

It is amazing that it is still there today. At some time it had been removed from its site and in about 1830 it was just given away by a churchwarden. The new owner realised its worth to the parish, returned it about 1855 and, through the efforts of the Essex Archaeological Society it was reset again in 1898.

Bradwell-on-Sea

There is a place in Essex where the past meets the present in glorious solitude. Go to Bradwell-on-Sea, take the road that heads towards Eastlands, park the car and walk the half-mile or so to St. Peter's chapel. You will be walking into history. This was probably the first church ever built on Essex soil. That was just after St. Cedd landed here in about A.D. 657 on his great campaign to convert the Saxons to Christianity. The historic significance of his little church was not appreciated as the centuries passed. It was demoted to use as a kind of lighthouse, for it stands right on the sea wall; then a farmer used it as a barn, until, in 1920 it was recognised for what it was, restored and reconsecrated.

St. Cedd chose a good spot for his church – the gateway of the old Roman fort which for centuries had defied not only the raiding Norsemen but also the storming rages of the North Sea. The fort is all gone now, but that tiny church still stands there. Stroll on the beach and scuffle the sand; you will find it is not made of ground-down rock, but of millions upon millions of shells broken down by the ceaseless fretting of the waves.

Look north east and you will see the great grey bulk of the Bradwell power station – a brooding, gentle giant which has provided electricity since 1963. Then look back at the church – in one glance you will have covered 1300 years!

St. Peter's Chapel, Bradwell-on-Sea

Braintree

The old town hall is now a heritage centre. It ought to be – for the very beauty of the murals which adorn its walls. And all this lovely example of harmony in architecture and art did not cost the ratepayers a penny. The town hall was erected and furnished at the expense of Sir William Courtauld to the design of Vincent Harris and opened in 1927. The striking bell of the clock in the tower was actually named Constance Cecily, after Sir William's wife. Was that not a nice thought?

A whole band of artists was assembled to beautify the rooms. The finest decoration of all must be the frescoes in the Council Chamber, painted by Maurice Greiffenhagen on copper plates which were then fixed to the walls. They portray some of the scenes in the fascinating story of Braintree from Roman times to modern days of farming and weaving, the area's principal industries.

It is worth an hour of anybody's time if ever they are round Braintree way. That hour will run into another if you look round the little museum so clearly displaying objects and the explanations of their role in the Braintree story. One man who gets a mention is Doctor Benjamin Allen. After 250 years of medical progress it is impossible for us to appreciate the state of medicine when he was one of Braintree's physicians, back in 1690. We can get some idea of what went on then in the surgery because Benjamin kept a rough notebook from 1723 in which he recorded some of his remedies, for future reference. After all, when he wrote them down they were the very latest ideas on the treatment of illnesses.

For one of his patients, poor old Mrs Luckin of Bocking he writes, 'I tried the bark and the common electuary' by which he means powdered quinine mixed up in a sweet substance like honey, to cure her of jaundice and the ague. It did not work. Then he adds, 'I would have had her take the Epsom salt and then gone to the waters at Tonbridge Wells, but Mr Dale, her acquaintance, opposed me and carried her away from sound advice'. It should be explained that Mr Dale was a rival Braintree doctor, so there was no love lost betweem them!

Benjamin Allen noted down another treatment for jaundice after the ague, a good old standby: slip a spoonful of powdered peacock's dung into a bitter drink – gulp it down – and you either got better – or worse. Tuberculosis sufferers were told to steep a pint of sheep's dung in a pint of milk overnight, then strain it off and drink it. Get bitten by a mad dog and the worthy doctor's remedy was: kill the dog, cut out its liver, fry it – and eat it. Was this the origin of that curious phrase for the cure of a hangover – 'The hair of the dog that bit you'?

At the beginning of this century Dr Harrison was the popular GP in Braintree. He was a great practical joker, the bane of the life of his family and friends. One of these friends was his neighbour in Bank Street, Frank Crittall, of metal windows fame. In the 1890s they supported opposing parties in the election. The Doctor, campaigning for the 'blue' Conservative faction, lured Frank's six-year-old son Valentine into his house, rigged him all out in blue, even dyed his face and hands, and took him round the town in his trap, canvassing support.

This was really going too far. Frank Crittall, strongly of the 'yellow' Liberal persuasion, got his own back. In the dead of night he and his friends painted the whole of Harrison's house, including windows, door and even the step itself, a loud and vivid yellow.

Brentwood

What chapel is more redolent of the drama of our Essex history than that old ruin of a church which stands amidst the chrome and concrete of modern materialism in Brentwood High Street? For example, we have heard recently of people seeking sanctuary in churches. There was just such a case here in this church back in 1232.

The man who headed for sanctuary then was Hubert de Burgh – a very important person. He had acted as Regent for the young King Henry III from 1216, and managed the country's affairs very well. But when the King came of age he turned on his trusty friend and ordered his trial on trumped-up charges. Three hundred soldiers were sent to capture him as he made his way towards London. They caught up with him in Brentwood, but he dashed into the chapel and, holding aloft the cross in one hand and the host, or communion bread, in the other he claimed sanctuary according to the ancient tradition.

The soldiers laughed at the very idea. They went in there and dragged him out and took him off to London. The Bishop of London was appalled at such sacrilege. He told the King he would excommunicate him and his troops for daring to defy the holy law. King Henry was crafty, he knew that sanctuary could actually be claimed for 40 consecutive days only, so he deferred to the Bishop, sent Hubert back to

Brentwood, made him comfortable in the church, then had his soldiers surround it – and wait. Poor old Hubert gave up, gave in, and was taken off to the Tower of London and imprisonment. It is nice to know that he was not executed, that part of his vast property was returned to him, and that he was freed to live in retirement for the last eleven years of his life.

The ruination of that chapel had begun well over 400 years ago. Back in 1577, Wistan Browne was Lord of the Manor and as wicked a squire as you would find in any Victorian melodrama. He owned all the land for miles around Brentwood, claimed that this old chapel belonged to him personally and ordered his men to start knocking it down. First they took the pulpit and the pews away, then the bell and the clock were lowered on to a cart and driven off.

It was the women of Brentwood who took action. They loved their church; they needed it. So they got together, 30 of them crowded into the chapel, locked and barred the door and threatened Squire Browne's men with a pathetic collection of weapons which included three bows and nine arrows and two kettles full of hot water. So the 'sit-in' is not as new an idea as one might think. Of course the women were soon overpowered and thrown into jail; but this disturbance came to the ears of the Privy Council. Browne was ordered to stop his desecration of the chapel – the brave women were freed. We have them to thank for the fact that the remains of that church still stand in the High Street, the brightest jewel in the crown of Brentwood's long history.

Brightlingsea

➤ The view of Brightlingsea which stays in my mind is the row of beach huts stretching all along the prom – so redolent of holidays of an earlier era, before the giant planes took holidaymakers to more certain sunshine. As the county handbook says, 'Brightlingsea is very much a "town of the sea" for its whole life is concerned with boating and fishing – and that includes oyster fishing'. Its significance as a port in former days was realised in 1984 when the British miners' strike brought shipload after shipload of foreign coal to be unloaded here in a haze of coal dust which covered the town while university students made a rowdy protest.

Its value as a port was recognised by its association with the port of Sandwich from so early a date that even in 1442 the ceremony of allegiance then enacted was said to date 'from time immemorial'. This ceremony fell into abeyance but was re-introduced in 1888 when a deputy was chosen to represent Brightlingsea, and to pay a token sum as a remembrance of the ships and men little Brightlingsea once placed at the service of its big brother Sandwich in time of war. It is still carried out, in the belfry of the old parish church of All Saints, nearly 100 ft up, looking out on a town which migrated more and more to the riverside, so that a new church of St James was built in 1837 down where all the action was.

All Saints, a good mile away inland, restored in recent years by a loving local band of 'Friends', has several points of interest. The most noticeable is the band of tiles all round the walls of the church – each tile inscribed with the names of Brightlingsea people lost at sea, wherever in the world they might have been, from 1872 down to 1962. The first tile says, 'This record commences from the time when Arthur Pertwee became vicar of this parish'. The second tells the sad story of David Day, lost with his schooner *William* on 9th December 1872. The tile which completed the circle remembers the day in August 1962 when a man on the *Sammy* was lost overboard. We owe the long continuation of this memorial to a legacy left by William Stammers, a former churchwarden.

Broomfield

Here is a church with an unusual feature and a delightful discovery. The feature is the round tower, one of the half a dozen such towers now surviving in Essex. It is around 900 years old now, built by the Normans, using a lot of Roman material robbed from ruins in the locality. The rest of the church reflects the care and repair of all the generations since, including a large amount of work on the north side in 1870.

A later restoration resulted in the discovery. A niche in a wall had been plastered over completely. Rebuilding exposed it and the treasure which was hidden in it – a Bible which had been the personal possession of King Charles I. Its value at that time had not been realised by the builders; it was cast upon the floor with a dozen or so other books to be disposed of – in a jumble sale, or even perhaps as rubbish. An old friend of the church, Colonel Lucas, of Witham, recounted how, on visiting the church for old times' sake, he saw these books lying higgledy-piggledy on the floor, picked one up and felt through its brown paper cover the embossing of letters on the binding.

He opened it and on the inside cover read this inscription: 'This Bible was King Charles the First's, afterwards was my grandfather's, Patrick Younge, Esq., who was library Keeper to his Majesty, now given to the Church at Broomfield by me, Sarah Atwood, Aug ye 4th, 1723'.

Younge lies buried under an inscribed slab of marble in the chancel. The inscription shows that one of his daughters was married to a John Atwood.

Another exciting discovery was made in this parish, nearer Chelmsford in 1894, when workmen digging for gravel came upon the remains of a Saxon burial. It waited for six years until the workmen were asked to dig gravel from this pit again before the burial was fully excavated. The finds were so rare and the arrangement so strange that it has been fully described in the Victoria County History, with a coloured illustration, and what was left of the inhumation has been preserved in the British Museum.

Burnham-on-Crouch

This yachting centre, patronised by the rich and the famous, is of international repute. Sailors set out from the quay to go boating in the river or to sail around the world. The Crouch is three-quarters of a mile wide here and there are more boats on the water than cars in the car parks. A walk along the quayside, which stretches the length of the town itself, is fascinating and invigorating. Five yacht clubs have their headquarters here in Burnham and the Burnham Week of racing and regattas is second only to Cowes. The future of yachting here has been assured through the purchase by the Crouch River Authority of all the rights in the river, thus preventing commercial development.

Pubs like the Queen's Head in the little alley called Providence, and the Victoria just off the quay at the other end of the High Street offer refreshment in the convivial company of seafaring folk. Burnham's great advantage is that there are no traffic snarl-ups because there is no through traffic. Near the Queen's Head in Providence there is a small museum established by volunteers and the local history society which tells the story of the town in particular and the area in general through objects and photographs collected over the years.

The old village of Burnham is centred on the church, which is just over a mile to the north beside the lane which runs east to places with nostalgic names like Dammers Wick and Twizzlefoot Bridge. The church is a strong, long-looking building, but it has had its catastrophes. The tower was blown down in the great storm of 1703, the spire in 1779, and a fire damaged the roof of the nave in 1774. The marriage register for that church covering the period from 1754 to part of 1774 is missing; the clue to its disappearance might be that it was taken out of the church safe for a wedding to be recorded on that very day of the fire – and was consumed.

Canvey Island

➤ It took a Dutchman to drain Canvey Island when it was nothing more than the largest of a series of islands of mud and silt shifting at the whim of the Thames and the tide. A syndicate of business men approached Cornelius Vermuyden, a Dutch engineer used to fighting the invasion of the sea into his own low-lying country. In 1623 he brought over his own team of men to embank this island, then drain it and make it fit for human habitation, with fields to be farmed.

The Dutchmen built their own houses, in their Dutch style, so that they could live on the job. Just two of them survive today. One was restored and opened in 1962 as the Dutch Cottage Museum in Canvey Road. In its two tiny rooms, one up and one down, artefacts and illustrations tell the story of this brave feat of land reclamation. The history of the island and its later development is also covered showing how good the grazing is for sheep and cattle and how the fair for their disposal was held here twice a year, with deals being done over a drink at the Lobster Smack, a charming old clap-boarded inn which claims its origin in 1563 and gets a mention by Dickens in *Great Expectations*.

Industry has largely ousted farming as the island's basic economy. People now pour in daily across the bridges to work here. The view of one end of the island is of structures, almost monumental, devoted to gas, oil and chemical en-gineering plants, but at the other end there is still enough solitude in the fields to encourage badgers to set up home. At the sea wall, specially raised to protect the island in the unlikely event of the lowering of the Thames Barrier, there is a close view of the fascinating variety of shipping up and down the estuary.

Castle Hedingham

➤ A lovely little town around a triangle of streets with a fascinating variety of architecture. Take just one as an ex-ample. The Bell Inn, as a building, was put up in the second half of the 16th century on an 'L' shaped plan which has been filled in and extended with modern extensions, making it a rambling public house today. Its deeds still surviving show that it was in business at least as early as 1730. In 1845 at the height of its importance it was called the Bell Com-mercial Inn and Posting House – the stage coach from Bury to London stopped here, bringing travellers and trade. But that was the year the trains came and the coaches made their last stop.

Tenants had to find other jobs to keep them going. In 1861 James Knight was publican and farmer. In 1882 the old brewhouse had been turned into a harness-maker's shop. From 1884 to this day the Bell has been owned by Grays who until recently supplied it from their brewery in Chelmsford.

The church of St. Nicholas has a grand Tudor tower, with a projecting stair turret under a small cupola, all in red brick. You have to go inside to see the best evidence of its building at the end of the 12th century. Look up at the amazing 'double hammerbeam' timber roof of the nave. One of only four such roofs in Essex churches, it fills one with awe and admiration of the skill of carpenters with such primitive tools.

The building above all to be visited, and it is open daily from May to October, is the castle. It was built in 1140 by Aubrey de Vere, son of one of William the Conqueror's leading supporters. It is one of the best preserved castle keeps in England, rising up to nearly 100 ft to the tip of its two square corner turrets. The bridge across the moat was built in 1496 to replace the original drawbridge. One of the pleasant things about a trip here is that the owners in their leaflet say, 'Families can enjoy the peace and quiet of these tranquil surroundings, and can picnic on the grass of the inner bailey'.

Chappel

➤ Chappel once had the charming name of Pontisbright. That was in the 11th century when Beorhtric, builder of the bridge (pons in Latin), or owner of the land, was probably still remembered with gratitude for providing a bridge over the Colne where formerly pedestrians had to wade a risky ford. It was in those days that a chapel was built here for the convenience of the growing number of worshippers who could not get across to Wakes Colne church when the river was in full flood after rain or snow.

The architect of the other bridge which crosses the river, the magnificent railway viaduct, is not remembered locally in any way at all. Yet this viaduct of 30 arches, the largest of them 75 ft high, required, by estimation some 7,000,000 bricks to carry the railway that short but essential 320 yards. It was the largest viaduct the Great Eastern Railway ever built and still holds the record as the biggest in East Anglia. It is surely strange that a huge, brick viaduct which must have been a great blot on the landscape when it was first put up in 1849 should now, when it is of no further use at all, be classified as an 'ancient monument' to ensure its preservation.

Its presence is now accepted as a mellowed feature which all can enjoy from a public footpath through pleasing meadows in a circular amble of two miles, returning to the green, overlooked by houses in attractive architectural variety beside the church of St. Barnabas. The thick stone walls of that church were raised back in 1352 and the building has been kept in repair ever since as witness the little timber belfry housing two bells under a modern spire.

If, on viewing that viaduct you feel a bit nostalgic for the

Chappel Viaduct

sound of steam and the smell of smoke, just cross the river to the old Chappel and Wakes Colne station and what a pleasant surprise you will get. The station has been practically reconstructed, to look as it did when the Marks Tey, Sudbury and Bury Branch line and the Colne Valley Railway took folk on to the main line to London and the coast. Old locomotives, steaming up regularly, and carriages which match them in age and atmosphere revive memories of smuts in the eye on Sunday School outings. At certain times there is a chance to have a short ride back into those dream days!

Chelmsford

➤ There are few corners of the county town which have stayed hidden from the prying eye of the developer through the last century. Those buildings which have survived, like

the Shire Hall and the cathedral have been well covered in guide books. But there is a monument to Victorian engineering which does get overlooked. Citizens see the brick piers and the high arches of the railway viaduct striding across river and road as something of a blot on the landscape. But the sheer daring and the brilliant engineering of these railway pioneers is being recognised and stations, bridges and viaducts are being seen as examples of industrial archaeology, to be preserved for the insight they give us into that great age of steam.

When one considers the oozing, yielding clay of the meadows where Can and Chelmer flow it is something of a miracle that the viaduct has stood firm for nearly 150 years. The architect made it as graceful as he could with the material he had to use – bricks, millions of them. The *Essex Chronicle* of 3rd March 1843 tells of the first 'Trip throughout the line' by a party of 20 men responsible for financing and laying the railway: '. . . After emerging from the cutting, a prominent feature of the works, the Cann viaduct presented itself – as fine a specimen of a work of the kind as is to be found upon any line in the kingdom. It consists of 18 arches, each of them of 30 ft span, and 44 ft in height, with massive wings to sustain the embankment at each end. Topped with a light and elegant iron parapet which is now in the course of erection, it forms a beautiful and picturesque object when viewed from the New London Road. A short embankment connects this with the Chelmsford viaduct, and in the erection of the two structures 10,400,000 bricks have been laid.

'The Chelmsford viaduct is a masterpiece in this department of railway works. The construction is of a peculiar nature, being a double line of arches, extending upwards of 800 ft . . . The station, as we have before stated, is a neat, elegant and light structure of timber, in which every accommodation is afforded for the public and the officers.'

We take travel by train so much for granted today that it is difficult to appreciate the great excitement occasioned by that first trip, graphically described in the same newspaper: 'About half past twelve o'clock the shrill whistle of the fiery visitant, and the rumble of the train which he so steadily bore up to the station, turned many a wondering eye in Chelmsford in that direction, and soon parties began to trip thitherward, to the desertion of the fireside or shop, and the emptying of mine hosts' inviting benches, to indulge in a little speculative curiosity on the snorting stranger . . .'

Chipping Ongar

'Twinkle, twinkle little star.
How I wonder what you are . . .'

➤ Yes, we all know the dear old nursery rhyme, but did you know that it was written by a girl called Jane Taylor who lived in Essex? The Taylor family was a most talented bunch. Father Isaac was a minister in the Congregational church and a very clever engraver, illustrating editions of the Bible, Shakespeare, Goldsmith and others. Mother Ann was the author of books on housewifery. Among their children were Ann, born in 1782, Jane born in 1783 and Isaac born in 1787.

In the service of the church they moved from Lavenham to live in Colchester from 1796 until 1811; then they moved to Ongar, living in Castle House and then on Peaked Farm in 1814. It was while they were living in Colchester, in 1806, that Jane, then 23, and her sister Ann had published their second book of poems, called *Rhymes for the Nursery*. This was when Jane's world-famous poem, 'Twinkle, twinkle . . .' first appeared. It caught the public imagination and was learned willingly and loved by infants at their mothers' knee wherever round the globe English was spoken.

But most of us never got beyond the first verse. There are five verses in all – and the last one goes like this:

'As our bright and tiny spark
Lights the traveller in the dark,
Though I know not what you are,
Twinkle, twinkle, little star.'

Jane Taylor died in 1824, aged just 41 and lies buried in the Congregational churchyard at Chipping Ongar. The sadness of the story is that Jane never married, so she had no children of her own to teach her nursery rhymes.

Colchester

➤ Holly Trees, the big, old house which shelters Colchester's museum of 'bygones' illustrating more recent history has a strange connection with the lost village of Markshall and with the church at Coggeshall. But you do not look inside the museum for that link – you have to look outside, at the creeper-covered side wall where a bench is thoughtfully provided. Behind that seat, up against the wall stands a row of tombstones. Decipher what you can and you will find that they all refer to a Honywood family.

Now, I had seven brothers and sisters. My mum lived to be the head of a family of 38 people. I thought that was pretty wonderful until I heard about Mrs Honywood. She was married when she was 16 years old, had 16 children and came to live in Essex in 1605 as a widow aged 77. She came here because her son Robert, then living in Kent, needed a bigger house for his family of 15 children, and he found just what he wanted in the Hall at Markshall – a hamlet on the road from Coggeshall to Earls Colne. A good son, he took his mother along with that big family and she lived happily with them until her death at the age of 93.

Meanwhile her other children were being just as fruitful as Robert. In fact Mrs Honywood's 16 children produced so many more children in their turn, who also had large families, that, even while she was still alive that grand old lady could claim 367 descendants. When they had family reunions there were more people in the Hall than in the whole of the rest of the parish! But the stream of life has hurried on, not just the Hall but the church and its yard, where so many of the family were buried have disappeared – demolished in the name of progress.

When the church was torn down in 1933 the tombstones and monuments to various members of the Honywood family had to be disposed of. It would have been a sin to send them to a builder's yard. Heads were scratched and a compromise was agreed. All the family stones which could be recovered were to go to the museum, even though they have to stand outside, but the very special monument to Mrs

Honywood herself was 'taken in' as it were, by Coggeshall church. It can still be seen there on the wall of the sacristy – a small reminder of a big family.

Copford

➤ The parish fronts the A12 trunk road from Marks Tey to Stanway. The houses have collected all along the old A12 now the B1408 because, in the days of coaches and horses there was plenty of trade with the travellers to enrich the inhabitants. It was here on the north side of the road, a furlong west of the Roman river that the windmill, a post mill, stood on its little hill. Robert Oliver was the miller down to 1733, then it changed hands several times before the Ely family took it on through most of the last century. In a terrific thunderstorm in July 1859 the mill was struck by lightning and extensively damaged. By 1900 nothing was left but the rotting, weatherboarded body, which was shortly afterwards completely demolished and in our time even its mound was levelled. Only the name of the inn, the Windmill brings back the memory of that monument of village self-sufficiency.

The real old centre of Copford is much further south where Copford Hall and the parish church stand in peaceful partnership while ribbon development has spread from the main road to Copford Green to the west. Travellers interested in art, architecture and history come from all over the world to see not only the remarkable architecture of the church of St. Mary the Virgin, but also its wonderful wall paintings.

Its architecture is largely of the original 12th century building. The only additions are a south aisle added in the 14th century and a bell turret possibly 100 years after that. For some reason now unknown the most remarkable feature, the stone vaulting of the nave and chancel, was removed and replaced by timberwork. The wall paintings are an astonishing survival, for they were part of the original decoration – a decoration, let it be said with a message for the vast majority of worshippers who could neither read nor write – a message which we modern, literate viewers, strangers to the gospel and its interpretation at that time, find hard to decipher, especially as time has laid its disfiguring hand here and there.

Cranham

➤ The rector, writing in 1839 said Cranham was 'very narrow and three miles in length, the population being scattered throughout the whole extent'. Now, as part of the populous London Borough of Havering, the rector in 1966, V. Paul Bowen wrote: '. . . in 1956 there were so many houses between St. Mary's Lane and the Southend Arterial Road that plans were made for the provision of a second church in the northern part of Cranham . . .'

This is a place of change; it has changed its name. In the distant past it was called Bishop's Ockendon because it was that part of old Ockendon owned by the Bishop of London. It has changed its church, the old one became so ruinous that it had to be demolished and the new All Saints rose on the old site in 1874. The Hall has also been rebuilt since the days when General James Oglethorpe lived there and worshipped at the church. He is Cranham's most famous son, though he was actually born in Godalming. He became Member of Parliament for Haslemere and through 32 years as an MP campaigned for prison reform. One way out for the poor prisoner of those days was settlement in the colonies with a clean sheet. Oglethorpe led an expedition to Georgia in 1732 and put in hand the building of the settlement of Savannah. While he was there the Spanish attacked Georgia during the War of Jenkin's Ear of 1739. Oglethorpe commanded the defence and routed them at the Battle of the Bloody Marsh. He came back to England in 1743, and, at 47 years of age courted and won Elizabeth Wright a young heiress who on her parents' deaths had come into Cranham Hall and Canewdon Hall estates.

Here at Cranham, after a couple more years in Parliament, Oglethorpe retired, and for 30 years lived peacefully with his wife on their estate, riding out over the fields, entertaining famous people of the day like Walpole, Goldsmith and Boswell who were his intimate friends, until his death in 1785. Since he had remained Governor of Georgia until 1752, having founded it originally, there is a steady stream of Americans to the parish church today to pay tribute at his monument, a tablet on the south side of the chancel and at the plaque which marks his last resting place, the family vault in the centre of the chancel.

Creeksea

➤ Of all the characters who enlivened the drama of life in Essex in the second half of the 18th century, Sir Henry Bate-Dudley was one of the most colourful. He lived at Bradwell Lodge, more recently the home of the late Tom Driberg, MP. He was parson, magistrate, sportsman, farmer and editor of a national newspaper all rolled into one. He was also an enthusiastic huntsman who had the strange distinction of being the only such huntsman ever to have been in at the kill of a fox on the roof of a church.

It happened like this; following his own pack of hounds he left his fellow huntsmen far behind as the fox ran and ran. It ended up in the churchyard of All Saints at Creeksea where it scrambled up an ivy-covered buttress, looking for sanctuary. A couple of hounds also made the perilous climb. Not to be outdone Bate-Dudley hauled himself up after them, and as his friends wearily straggled in he swore that he had been in at the kill right there on the roof of the chancel.

He died in 1824, aged 79, by which time All Saints was going into a decline. It was rebuilt in 1878 in stone of various hues, in a romantic village church style very typical of Frederick Chancellor, the Chelmsford architect who achieved a greater place in Essex history by becoming the first Mayor of Chelmsford upon its incorporation as a borough in 1888. Look carefully and you can see that some of the Norman zig-zag decoration of the old church has been incorporated in the wall of the new.

From the church, just north of the golf course, it is quite a step to the river Crouch, but it is well worth it to enjoy the sights and sounds of this isolated spot in the peace of a mid-week morning. By the weekend the boat people are out and about!

Dagenham

➤ Dagenham has been part of the London borough of Barking for 24 years, but it was a village, then a borough in the county of Essex through more than 1,000 years, described 100 years ago as, 'A long, straggling village near the Thames . . . The church has been almost wholly rebuilt in a very unsightly style . . .' In those days this village still had a wide marshy foreshore to the Thames, right where the great Ford factory now stands. The pool of water behind it is a lingering reminder of a catastrophe which occurred on 17th December 1707.

An extra high tide, with the wind behind it, came surging up the river. A sluice-gate broke open under the pressure. As Captain John Perry says in his *Account of the Stopping of Dagenham Breach* published in 1721, it 'might, if proper and immediate Help had been apply'd, have been easily stop'd with a small Charge . . . but through the Neglect thereof, the constant Force of the Water setting in and out of the Levels, soon made the Gap wider . . .' The breach widened to 100 yards and the water lay 20 ft deep. Thousands of acres were flooded in a creek which ran almost up to the village. The silt washed out on the ebb tide made such a sandbank in the Thames that it interfered with the passage of shipping.

Parliament was perturbed, it voted a special tax on all traffic up the Thames to raise money for repairs. But contractors, though willing, were beaten by the sheer force of the flood. William Boswell said he could mend it for £16,500 but in the end he had to admit defeat. For eight years the flood ran free, then, in 1715 Captain Perry put his experience at the service of the country. In five years, and with a great band of workmen he did achieve the closing of the reach, at a cost of £40,472 18s 8¾d. Since he had undertaken to do it for £25,000 plus a further grant from the government if this became necessary, and because that further grant was

£15,000 it can be seen that poor Captain Perry actually had to pay for his success.

The great bulk of the Ford factory could be considered a massive memorial to Captain Perry – it would never have been there but for Perry's persistence.

Danbury

➤ Essex changes all the time, but people stay the same. Let me explain. Danbury Palace, now a county council conference centre was once the home of a bishop, when Essex was in the diocese of Rochester. During the last war it was a maternity home. Long, long ago there was no house there at all; it was the deer park belonging to St. Clere's Hall on the other side of the road. King Henry VIII granted it all to his brother-in-law William Parr, and he, hardly believing his luck, sold it straight away to the local squire, Sir Walter Mildmay.

He it was who built the first house here and called it Danbury Place. The tax return which listed how many fireplaces each house had, for which a tax must be paid, showed that there were no fewer than 16 in this great house. Sir Humphrey Mildmay, born in 1593, lived here in great style. But he backed the Royalists in the Civil War, so he had to lie low through the Commonwealth period. He stayed at home, drinking and gambling with the rector, Clement Vincent, who had been thrown out of the living by the Puritans. They also seized Mildmay's lands and he had to pay more than £1,000 to get them back.

He kept a diary of the times. One entry shows just how human he was. In 1641 he wrote: 'After dinner my woman and I did fall out ill-favourdly and so we both continued sulky till worthily I did acknowledge all error to be mine, when all became well again and we to supper and Bedd.' Men are still writing entries like that today!

After his death Danbury Place passed through several hands, the estate split up until the dilapidated old house was reduced to the status of a mere farmhouse. Then John Round bought it, in 1831, pulled it all down and built the present

55

Danbury Palace

house now known as Danbury Palace. He employed the famous architect Thomas Hopper, but his wife Susan also had a lot to do with the design, not only to make it as picturesque as possible but also to make sure that three staircases were installed, one of them entirely of stone, for she had a great fear of being trapped in a fire.

Poor woman, she did die in a fire. She and her husband had gone to stay in a London hotel. The fire alarm sounded. Susan thought she had time to dash upstairs and retrieve a valuable bracelet, but she was trapped in the fire and the smoke. John Round brought her body back to lie in a grave in Danbury churchyard which is still marked. He could not bear to live in the house without her. He put it up for sale in 1845 and it was bought by the church to serve as the Palace for the Bishop of Rochester whose diocese then included Essex. A beautiful chapel was built on to the Palace. Then the diocese boundaries were revised, Essex was excluded, the Bishop moved and the Palace was sold in 1892. The new owner is said to have cut down no less than 429 oak trees to realise their value as timber, and the character of the old Place or Palace was changed beyond recognition.

The beautiful lakes which formed part of the early gardens are now in the public domain, with a car park in amongst the trees.

Debden

➤ I like Debden, its steep little hills, its houses tucked away in greenery. The church, too, is hidden away down the narrowest of lanes – a cul-de-sac, and at the end of it such peace and such beauty in a wilderness which once was part of Debden Hall estate.

In the church were married, in 1733, Peter Muilman, described as a gentleman of St. Botolph extra Bishopsgate and Mary Chiswell a considerable heiress. He made a fortune as a London merchant and died in 1790. Their son came into the possession of Debden Hall and a fortune of £120,000 from his mother's side of the family and from his father he inherited £350,000 – imagine what value that would represent today! He had Debden Hall rebuilt and restored the church which had been ruined when the tower fell, not once but twice, in 1698 and 1717. He also gave the new font. But rich as he was he could not come to terms with life. He shot himself in Debden Hall on 3rd February 1797.

Some people have said that he worked with his father in producing *A New and Complete History of Essex* published in 1770 under the pseudonym of 'A Gentleman' in several volumes liberally illustrated. Doubt has been cast on Muilman's authorship; he may well have been the sponsor or patron who guaranteed the publication against possible loss. One copy of the work has had added, at the end of the title-page 'By Sir Henry Bate Dudley'. He was a man who proved his literary skill as editor of the *Morning Post* from 1775, so this addition, in a contemporary hand could well state the truth of the matter.

For 100 years Debden was a prosperous estate of nearly 5,000 acres, then it went through several hands, the old Hall became a white elephant – it was demolished and the land was dispersed in 1935.

The forgotten tragedy of Debden was the day in 1904 when a March gale blew a spark from a chimney on to the thatched roof of a cottage. It blazed and set light to the thatch of the house across the road. How that fire roared – twelve houses were destroyed and 'Great panic prevailed among the villagers who cleared their houses'. Over 50 homeless people took refuge in the school and in neighbours' houses. Lord Strathcona, who owned most of Debden telegraphed his bailiff to open the Hall and his farms to the refugees. All that fear, all that loss, all forgotten.

Dedham

➤ A great place for a day out with historical associations to look up, architectural beauty to look at, a craft centre with bargains to look into and countryside so inspiring that it has been captured on canvas by one of our greatest English painters.

John Constable crossed the Stour every day to come to school in Dedham. Looking back in adulthood he said, 'I love every stile and stump, and every lane in the village . . .' He expressed that love in paintings like Dedham Vale and Dedham Lock which, in countless editions of reproductions, are proudly hung on walls of houses all around the world. Yet it was not until he was 52, in 1828, when his father-in-law left him £28,000 that he could at last, as he said, 'stand before a six-foot canvas with a mind at ease, thank God'.

We can walk in his footsteps down to the lock – though we must accept changes – the mill on the Stour here is now a block of prestigious flats, but the water meadows are still there, where we can wander, finding Constable's peace of mind, recharging our spiritual batteries just as he did.

The architecture on view must include the church, a real beauty, built through the piety of merchants made rich in the cloth industry which was thriving in Essex in the 15th century. By the time the whole church was built, over 30 years from 1492 the woollen trade was declining. So, just in time, St. Mary's was built, and has been kept in repair for us to appreciate 500 years later. Perhaps we should say a small prayer at the monument to the Webbe family, for it was they with the Gurdons who largely financed its erection.

The house opposite, Shermans, is owned by the National Trust. It sports an unusual sundial high up in the centre of the parapet, but this is only a minor feature in appreciating the early Georgian facade. There are so many more interesting old houses on the way through the town to the Dedham Arts and Crafts Centre in the converted Congregational church. All kinds of local craftsmen and women put their wares on view for sale and there is a toy museum which shows objects from round the world and down the ages.

Last, but not least, at Castle House the studio of that well-known modern artist, Sir Alfred Munnings, is kept just as it was when he was at the height of his power. He, like Constable, found inspiration in the beauty of Dedham and its environs which helped him cope with the difficulties of the office of President of the Royal Academy to which he was elected in 1944. His studio has to be looked for about half a mile out of Dedham itself.

Dengie

➤ Dengie is as much a geographical location as a village. It had more inhabitants when farming needed men and horses. Now it is a quiet place where roads peter out on the Dengie Marshes. Cart tracks and footpaths give access to the sea wall at a centre point for walks to Bradwell to the north and Burnham to the south. The quality of light, the grand skyscapes and the cries of the wild birds on the saltings and out across Dengie Flat are the attractions – a fine day is the catalyst which turns it all into sheer delight.

After such a walk absorbing the atmosphere one can read in armchair comfort the books by S. L. Bensusan, a journalist who came to live here in 1908 and fell in love with the place and the people. His *Countryside Chronicle*, *Marshland Voices*, *Marshland Calling* and so on, bring back agreeably to mind memories of our own ramblings.

Daniel Defoe disliked Dengie; he caught a nasty fever out there on the marshes while travelling around to compile his *Tour Through Great Britain* published in 1722. Sidney Tiffin, a Tillingham man paddling his punt after wild fowl on the water in October 1949 caught something much more unpleasant. It was the corpse, minus head and legs, of Stanley Setty a London car dealer. Donald Hume was alleged to have killed him, cut him up, wrapped up the bits in parcels, then dropped them from an aeroplane over the Dengie Marshes. The jury could not agree at his trial. The final outcome was that Hume was given a twelve-year sentence for being an accessory to the murder.

Downham

➤ Downham did not see the Romans marching and it is not recorded in the Domesday Book under that name. It first appears as 'Dunham' in the Red Book of the Exchequer of 1168, and as Dounham in property deeds from the 13th century, when Barn Hall is mentioned.

In the next century we can read of another property, belonging to the de Hemenhale family – and it was still called Fremnells 600 years later when the water in the Hanningfield reservoir slowly rose to obliterate all evidence of its existence. In 1768 it was described as, 'The mansion house is a large old building, lying in a bottom, above a mile and a half north from the church. 'Tis vulgarly called Frimnells.' It was held, as the Manor of Hemnales, by Sir Thomas Tyrell up to his death in 1476. In 1683 Sir Thomas Raymond died in possession of it and was buried under an altar tomb in the church. Two centuries later the manor house had been reduced to the state shown in the sale catalogue of 1867: 'An ancient MANSION, now occupied as a Farm House'. By 1937 Fremnells had resumed its status as a nice place in the country, lived in then by a local Justice of the Peace, Lawrence Kirk.

In 1954 Nikolaus Pevsner, writing in his *Buildings of England* series, states that the house as he saw it dated from about 1630 and was built on an E plan. It had those stone-mullioned windows which make an English country house so handsome. He concludes 'It is said that the house is to be submerged by the Hanningfield reservoir. That would be a thousand pities, as it is the best house of its date in Essex'. A footnote to the 1965 edition simply says, 'It has been submerged'.

It must be said that since the Hanningfield scheme, completed in 1956, the county has never been short of water, and the 354 hectares of the reservoir have the beauty of a lake, with marginal lands planted with conifers and hardwoods. Birds and butterflies are attracted, wild flowers have crept back. One section is a bird sanctuary with only limited access. The best view of the reservoir and that sanctuary is from the Wickford-Stock road to the south.

Earls Colne

William the Conqueror gave his faithful retainer Aubrey de Vere any number of Saxon manors. One of them was called Cheaping because it already had the licence to hold a market. Aubrey's descendants were created Earls of Oxford, so this place Cheaping, on the river Colne, took that title as part of its name, and Earls Colne it has since been called. It is a pleasant place in which to live, as witnessed by the number of fine houses in spacious grounds which can be seen here.

One of them is Colne House. Whilst he owned it, some 25 years ago, Mr Arthur Evans, specialist electrical engineer and manufacturer of light cells, commissioned its history. He found it all began with Osgood Gee who, like his wife, was born in 1795. They were married in 1821 and first set up house in Ashford Lodge, here in the village. By 1837 Osgood was dead, and since both their daughters had died in their youth Mary Gee was left widowed and childless, lonely but for the company of her valued companion. She was rich and had already used her money to benefit the locality. For example, she had backed the setting up of a charity school in Great Malpestead in about 1836 and she provided a purpose-built, village school there in 1863. In 1838 she founded an infants school in Earls Colne itself.

At the same time she put in hand the building of a new house, probably finding Ashford Lodge too depressingly full of memories. It was to be called Colne House, and it was ready for occupation by 1840. Unknown to her a tile unseen behind the fireplace had scratched upon it, 'Mr. Ward built this house and he broke before he built it, 1840.' Poor man, he had built such a beautiful house, with no less than 13 bedrooms. Mrs. Gee lived here with her companion, Elizabeth Barter, the schoolmistress of her school and her six servants until she died on Christmas Eve 1864. By then her benefactions had also included more than two thirds of the cost of building the church of the Holy Trinity at Halstead and the whole cost of erecting St. James at Greenstead Green in 1845.

Her nephew, Lt. Col. Frederick Marsden then occupied Colne House for 20 years or more followed by George W. Taylor and sometime later, by Lt. Gen. Sir Alfred Roberts. The military connection was continued when, in 1937 the county directory showed Lt. Col. A. A. Soames there and he it was who sold it to Arthur Evans in 1946. He was well-known in the locality as member and, for three years, chairman, of the Halstead Urban District. Prior to the Second World War he wrote to Winston Churchill, pointing out the virtual monopoly by the Germans of the manufacture of the photocell and the problems it might cause if war broke out. It was Churchill's encouraging reply which caused Arthur Evans to do something about it himself. He set up Evans Electroselenium and by the time war did come he was exporting photocells in competition with the Germans.

As to the house, he made a number of tasteful improvements. He resurrected the garden from what had degenerated into wartime potato patches to a beautiful display of green lawns and colourful flower beds, creating a rock garden over which an artificial stream gurgled, endlessly replenishing itself through an invisible underground duct. When Arthur Evans moved to the Channel Islands in the late 1960s he was very much missed.

Now let it be said that half a dozen houses in Earls Colne could be chronicled in this manner, with the school and the church yet to be mentioned! The church was much restored in 1884, but the windows in the south aisle prove its origin in the 14th century. The story of Earls Colne Grammar School has been comprehensively told by A. D. Merson in his history published by the governors of the school in 1975, from its foundation in 1520 to its closure in 1883 and its re-opening four years later, down to that fateful day in 1972 when a girl was admitted for the first time.

East Hanningfield

➤ What satisfaction there must be in digging for water and eventually finding it. We refer, of course, to the days when water was a scarce commodity, to be collected from a well or pond which might be miles away. The idea of having water on your land, let alone from a tap over a stainless steel kitchen unit, was just a dream to most villagers in the 18th century. Even the parson at East Hanningfield did not have this useful perquisite until he set the work in hand himself – and what an arduous task it turned out to be. So difficult and unusual was it that it came to the attention of the national press. Here is what a reader said, writing to *The Gentleman's Magazine* on 8th July 1791:

'Unacquainted as I am with the measurement of the deepest wells in this kingdom, I conjecture the one at length fortunately completed by the Rev. Mr. Nottidge, at East Hanningfield parsonage, near Chelmsford, to be sufficiently extraordinary to merit your notice. It was begun June 21, 1790, and water, when the workmen, from such tedious labour, were at the moment of despair, was found May 7, 1791. Thirty-nine thousand five hundred bricks were used, without cement, in lining this well, the soil of which, for the first 30 feet, was a fine, light-brown, imperfect marl; and though fossils may ingeniously choose to discriminate the different strata, yet, except from shades of a deeper colour and firmer texture, occasionally, but slightly, mixed with a little sand and a few shells, the same soil, to a common eye, without more material variation, continued to 450 feet, where it was consolidated into so rocky a substance as to require the being broken through with the mattock. A bore then, of 3 inches diameter and 15 feet in length, was tried, which soon, through a soft soil, slipped from the workman's hands and fell up to the handle. Water instantly appeared, and rose within the first hour 150 feet, and, after a very gradual rise, now stands at 347 feet, extremely soft and well-flavoured . . .'

The parson had dug the well for the benefit of his parishioners, 'for whose use it is always open' he declared. A good man.

They benefited from water – but suffered by fire; the church was burnt down on 5th January 1884. That fire brought to light under coats of lime wash some most amazing and exquisite wall paintings done around A.D. 1300. The vicar tried to protect them behind glazed doors, but vandals broke them. In 1933 it was reported that the expert, Professor Tristram, had successfully peeled one portion of these paintings from the wall for preservation in the Victoria and Albert Museum together with accurate drawings of those he was unable to remove.

The church we now see was built in record time. Work started on 16th July 1884 and it was consecrated on 16th June 1885 – and all done by manual labour.

East Horndon

In 1695 John Tyrell of Billericay wrote down a story told him by his great grandfather, Sir Henry Tyrell of Heron in Essex, who had heard it at his grandfather's knee. It goes like this:

'Merchants who traded with tribes in faraway Africa brought home a great serpent. When the ship anchored at last in the Thames the serpent escaped from its cage and swam ashore, creeping into the woods which then covered the land between Heron and Horndon parish church. The rumour grew that it preyed on travellers along the road, swallowing them whole. Sir James Tyrell was not knighted for nothing! He took on the mantle of St. George. Early one morning he donned his armour, had his servant fetch his sword and then he hung a large mirror round his neck, facing forward. He took up his position beside the serpent's lair. Out popped the dreaded snake, saw his reflection in the mirror and just for a moment was quite taken aback. In that moment Sir James upped with his sword, slew the serpent, cut off its head, carried it home and presented it to his wife whilst she still lay in bed.

'But he had worked himself up so much in killing the serpent that he collapsed and died. Some time later his son,

64

still mourning, came upon the place where the creatures' bones still lay. He kicked them viciously as he cried, "These are the bones of the serpent which killed my father!" One bone pierced his shoe, pricked his toe; gangrene set in and he had to have his leg cut off at the knee.' Old Heron Hall which once stood where Heron House is in East Horndon had a window in which the portrait of this one-legged man was shown in stained glass.

The village of East Horndon can hardly be identified today. Its church on the hill is cut off from it by the interminable rush of traffic on the main road; but it was so little used that it was declared redundant. About 20 years ago its bells were stolen by a gang which ripped holes in the roof to get them out. Local volunteers restored it and nowadays it is used for art exhibitions and music workshops.

Elmstead Market

This was the place where the elm trees grew when the pioneers made it their home. But why was Market added? This suffix was being used as early as 1495 to distinguish this settlement from Elmstead proper, a good mile to the north. The next question then is why should a new village have been established in such close proximity to the old one? Some say that a visitation of the plague so terrified the traders that they would not go near, but set up their stalls down here on the highway. Others contend that it was the growing number of travellers on that highway from Harwich through Colchester to London which made the villagers migrate down there to turn an honest penny in a market granted by Henry III in 1253.

Whatever it was, the church was left behind and stands there today within sight and sound of the new main road, the A120, which means that Elmstead Market is the more peaceful of the two places. St Lawrence's has many architectural features to be enjoyed, from a Norman doorway to the fine south chapel of the 14th century, but what really catches the imagination are two very different monuments. One is a rare, life-sized effigy of a Knight Templar, a Crusader who came back, carved in oak by an unknown crafts-man seven centuries ago. The other is a brass, showing just two hands holding in their palms a heart inscribed with one word: 'Credo' – I believe. It was made about 1500 and its message of faith has touched the hearts of generations.

The modern place to be visited in this parish is the Beth Chatto Gardens. At White Barn House one can see plants growing in any number of different habitats , giving us ideas for those difficult corners of our own gardens; and in the nursery there is a chance to buy those plants – then it is home to the fork and the trowel!

Epping

Epping grew up as a settlement in the forest – a first or last stop on the way to and from the great city of London. Its long main street still shows the architecture of such a stop-ping-place, with inns and arches over alleyways to stables at the rear, one or two larger houses of London merchants and later developments like the shops and the churches of developing religions such as the Friends' Meeting House. The parish church did not get built until 1909 when its tower, separate from nave and aisle, completed a building of style which was then furnished with taste. The really old church for the area is All Saints at Epping Upland, the old parish of which Epping was once but a hamlet. It was built in the 13th century.

The forest shrank back from Epping as it was used for building timber and for fuel by the growing town, but it was still the place for jolly jaunts out from smoky, crowded London. Thomas Hood, celebrated poet and humorist tells, in 1830, of his view of the annual outing to join in the famous Epping Easter Chase:

'Epping for butter justly fam'd,
And pork in sausage pop't,
Where winter time, or summer time,
Pig's flesh is always chop't.

The ruins of Copped Hall, Epping

But famous more, as annals tell,
Because of Easter Chase;
There ev'ry year, 'twixt dog and deer,
There is a gallant race.'

Hood adds: 'I attended the last Anniversary of the festival, and am concerned to say that the sport does not improve, but appears an ebbing as well as an Epping custom . . .'

The hunt Hood describes was a comical, noisy disaster. Today more sober expeditions can be made to savour historical sites widely differing in period but in close proximity to Epping. A mile out of town towards London on the B1393 (formerly the A11) is a banked enclosure by the road on the left-hand side opposite the lane to Upshire. This is Ambresbury Banks. Some historians believe that behind this inadequate rampart Boadicea, or Boudicca, and her faithful British tribesmen took up their last stand against the might of the Roman army in A.D. 62 and were annihilated. The forest wreaths the spot in green remembrance.

Copped Hall is best approached on foot along a path from that lane to Upshire, Along a hedgerow with beautiful views to the east, the path is carried over the M25 on a bridge which sees that river of rushing traffic from an unusual viewpoint. The walk is the most important part of the visit, for the Hall is now a roofless ruin, destroyed in a terrible fire in 1917. Its beauty of white brick against the verdant woods and before the rippled lake is gone but there is a lingering atmosphere of the famous and the wealthy who called this place home from its building in 1753. Long before that there was a house on this site. Princess Mary, later Queen Mary I was living here in 1551 when the Privy Council ordered that she should cease having the Roman Catholic mass celebrated here in the secrecy of the enveloping forest.

Faulkbourne

How irritating for motorists and for walkers! This place needs two of the O.S. 1:50 000 maps; on sheet 168 you find the Hall with the church to the west on the extreme left-hand edge of the map. The village street has to be looked for on map 167 on the right-hand edge, south east of Black Notley. The spot I like best, largely for its place in the legendary history of Faulkbourne is the pond at the edge of the road between Home Farm and the church. Though not shown on the map this is a pond of great significance, for it is fed by a spring which was in the earliest times considered a holy well, long before the Saxons were converted to Christianity. The god of water, the giver of life lived in this holy well. It is most likely that the present church was sited in this spot because it was the accredited holy place of the pagan gods.

Even into medieval times the spring was thought to have healing powers which attracted pilgrims. It was called St. German's Well and the church is dedicated to the same missionary bishop. In it one can trace through the architecture of the nave and the chancel, its origin in Norman times. The Hall, which stands close by, has been declared the finest 15th century mansion now existing in the county, carried out in warm, red brick, even to its towers, turrets and battlements.

Look out for the old post office just a little further up the street. The sign on the wall of the house has been painted out because it no longer provides that service. Notice under the bedroom window a small shutter still in position after 200 years. It was fixed there by an enterprising postmaster. When the Witham mail coach came clattering through the village on an early winter's morning the poor old postmaster had to creep down-stairs in his nightshirt and open his door to frost and snow as he took in the mail for the village. Since mail coaches were pretty tall affairs the postmaster built this little hatch through the wall beside his bed. The coachman had only to tap on it with his whip and the postmaster could open it, take in his letters and still stay snug and warm. How civilised! Let us hope future owners will know the story and preserve this fascinating feature.

Felsted

➤ A small enough place, but it has certainly left footprints in history. The first one, from a very long time ago, is recalled by the celebration of the 900th anniversary of the Domesday Book. It is a very hard book to read in that it lists in great detail and in very obscure language all the classes of people in every town and village in our county – all their fields, their mills, their fisheries, their animals, even their bees. All this information was gathered together to show William the Conqueror the value of the land he had taken over.

All very serious you might say; but there's one entry in the Essex section of the Domesday Book which shows us that those Normans were as fond of a joke as we are. To appreciate their joke you should first look in the telephone directory under the name Godsalve, Godsave or Godsafe. You'll see a lot of entries of a family name which goes all the way back to that Domesday Book. It sounds a very religious and holy name – but look under Felsted in that book and you will see that the King had given land there to one of his naughty Norman knights, written down in the Domesday Book as 'Roger God-save-the-ladies'! It is not surprising, then, that he had quite a few descendants!

Come down another 400 years and the second footprint is the amazing monument in the church under which lies buried Richard Rich. An apt name, for he made himself one of the richest men in the country. He was born in 1500; by the time he was 48 he had become Lord Chancellor and was handling vast sums of money on behalf of the King in the acquisition and resale of monastic property. He obtained Leez Priory for himself and so came to live in Essex with the title 1st Baron Rich of Leez Priory. For another 20 years he kept his head while those about him were losing theirs, serving a succession of sovereigns and retiring to Leez. He had a number of estates in Essex and died at one of them, Rochford Hall.

It was he who founded Felsted school in 1564, so it is not unreasonable that he should choose this church in which to be buried. Yet it was not his son who had the grand monument set up. That had to wait until around 1620 when his grandson put in hand a magnificent memorial in multi-coloured marbles, 15ft high showing Lord Rich at rest with his son, who died in 1581, kneeling in prayer, backed by a group of figures in high relief representing Wisdom, Truth, Justice, Fortitude, Hope and Charity, all placed under a canopy supported by two bronze columns. The work is of the highest order, probably by the famous Epiphanius Evesham.

For all the grandeur of that tomb there was a humble craftsman whose name is more immediately in the public eye. Look along the bressumer, the main horizontal beam supporting the upper floor of the house opposite Lord Rich's original school and you can read the message, 'George Boot made this house, 1596'. Wouldn't he be proud to think that it was standing still, after 400 years? It makes an exclusive restaurant today where one can call for a bottle of the local brew, wine from the Felstar Vineyard at nearby Cricks Green.

Finchingfield

➤ This is the village I call the Calendar Queen of Essex. In every Essex calendar you buy there is always a shot of the pond and the steep hill beyond it leading up to the church. It is such a picturesque place that it deserves that title; and what with the timber-framed Guildhall under which one passes to the church with its sturdy Norman tower and the old windmill under restoration just around the corner, together with inns which offer meals and a couple of antique shops for good measure, it is not surprising that parking on a summer Sunday is difficult for tourists and inhabitants alike.

Look for Spains Hall, down the side road, when it offers an open day in aid of charity. A great friend of Essex, its former Lord Lieutenant, Sir John Ruggles-Brise, lets people roam his gardens, pointing out the lakes which are the subject of a strange story.

William Kempe was born here in 1555, had a happy

childhood, married and saw his daughter happily married while he stayed here in Spains Hall. One day, in the course of a silly tiff, he accused his wife of being unfaithful. He knew she never had been, and he regretted his words so much that he there and then made a vow that he would not speak again for seven whole years. He wrote orders to his servants – but how his wife must have suffered through this rigid silent self-punishment! Folklore has it that for every year that passed he had a large fishpond dug out in his garden. Even when his wife died in 1623 he kept his vow of silence.

It is said that, in 1628, at the end of his seven years of silence he tried to speak again, and found he could not utter a sound. The shock killed him! You can read his memorial, in Latin, in the south aisle of the church.

Foxearth

➤ We are told by the district guide that this, 'is a pleasant old-world village with a restored Elizabethan mansion complete with moat and a quite imposing church with rich wall paintings, and painted panels in the rood screen'. What is missed is the unusual establishment here of a brewery, way out in the countryside, miles away from any great centre of population to drink its product. Foxearth lies right on the border of Essex with Suffolk, north of the three Belchamp villages. A hundred years ago there were 300 inhabitants and that went down to 288 before the last war. Hardly enough people to keep a pub going, let alone a brewery.

It started off as something more common than a pub – a simple beerhouse. Back in 1859 George Ward was a beer retailer. He made the beer in his house and the villagers went into what would have been his front room with their bottles and jugs, to take home a pint or two. They may well have sat down for a moment to rest their feet and take a glass of ale straight from the barrel while they exchanged local news and gossip. They liked George's beer, it tasted good, they came back for more.

When George passed on some 20 years later his widow

Charlotte came into her own. Seeing that George's beer was so popular locally she looked at ways of selling it over a wider area. She kept on the beerhouse, but expanded the beer-making into a brewery capable of much greater production. Her son came into the business with her, and what a go they made of it! Charlotte set on its feet a company which continued as Ward & Son Ltd down to 1956 when it was taken over by Taylor Walker, the big combine, and continued simply as a depot. The old brewhouse has been demolished and there is no memorial standing to the grit of that Victorian lady who entered the male domain of brewing and showed them the way to do it.

Galleywood

Galleywood Common, south of Chelmsford on the B1007 is a lovely open space where one can park the car for nothing, have picnics, fly kites and just mess about generally. If you had been driving down the Stock road in 1935 you would have been held up on race days while the horses galloped down the hill, turned across the road and struggled up the hill again to the finish. There was a racecourse here from at least 1750. It was so well-known that King George III gave two prizes of 100 guineas to be raced for, and they were continuously presented from 1759 down to 1876. In 1890 the course was replanned and a big, new grandstand was built.

Fashions changed, flat-racing gave way to steeplechasing, held twice a year over two days. The gentry rode on the first day and farmers and tradesmen who fancied their chances as amateur jockeys competed on the second day. That stopped, largely from lack of support, in 1935 when pony racing was introduced. The war put a stop to that, and after five years of enforced neglect the course was never reinstated.

It had a connection with the last man to be hanged in Chelmsford Gaol. On the course, and used as a stand on race days was a pub called the Admiral Rous, named after the famous sporting admiral who had it built originally as his own private grandstand. Here Samuel Crozier comes into the picture. He was a publican who once kept the Globe at

Rainsford End in Chelmsford. His first wife died in a mental hospital; then he met Cecilia, barmaid at the Fleece in Duke Street. He was then unemployed, but together they put in for the licence of the Admiral Rous, obviously a good little earner on race days.

But Crozier was already addicted to the bottle and his drunken bouts made him aggressive and very cruel. After the pub was closed at night there were few people living near enough to hear the rows. Cecilia had nowhere else to go. Patrons of the pub saw the signs of the beatings her husband gave her. After months of this cruelty she was reduced to a shadow of her former cheerful self, a woman too weak to offer resistance, and this seemed to inflame the drunken bully all the more. He went too far one night; threw her down on the floor so hard that she struck her head against it, and never got up again. Crozier was tried, found guilty of murder and so achieved a niche in the hall of history as the last man to be hanged in the prison at Chelmsford.

Gestingthorpe

In the tower, added to the Norman church of St. Mary around 1498 there is a message; with hindsight a message of sadness and regret. The fifth and sixth bells are inscribed: 'In gratitude to God for the safe return with honour of my beloved son from the dangers of war in South Africa'.

That son was Lawrence Edward Grace Oates. He grew up in Over Hall, better known today as Gestingthorpe Hall, in the 1880s. He was a frail boy, sent on sea voyages to improve his health, who grew up with a passion for horses. Age brought strength. At 20 years old he was a subaltern with the Inniskilling Dragoons. In December 1900 he stepped ashore in Cape Town and was immediately sent into action against the Boers. His bravery earned promotion to Lieutenant, and subsequent daring feats in action earned him the nickname 'No surrender Oates'. After a particularly bad injury he returned to Gestingthorpe to convalesce – the reason for the inscription on the bells.

To cut a long story short Oates got special leave from his regiment to join the famous Captain Robert F. Scott in his attempt to reach the South Pole. It was an ill-fated expedition. By 16th January 1912 they were just 27 miles short of the Pole. They saw the tracks which showed them that Amundsen had beaten them to it. They struggled on to the Pole just to say that they had made it. On the fearful fight back to their base camp Oates, already badly frostbitten, became desperately ill. He knew he was holding back the small band's attempt to reach safety. He purposely walked out of the tent into a blizzard saying, 'I am just going outside, I may be some time'. Of course he never came back. The date was 17th March 1912 – his birthday. Essex, and Gestingthorpe, are proud of him. There is a brass on the north wall of the church which records this last act of bravery. The visitor who reads it can look up to a nave roof erected 500 years ago of a double-hammerbeam construction – complicated, beautiful and rare in our county.

The Hall which sheltered the mourning mother of Captain Oates is still there, showing its 18th century architecture, but it does not seem all that old after hearing that Roman remains were discovered on Hill Farm from 1950 onwards. Pottery with a French potter's mark, a dagger, a chisel, a brooch and pieces of millstone were just some of the items recovered, proving that a sophisticated Roman family lived here through 400 years in some comfort, right down to central heating, with a stokehold and ducts for the circulation of warm air.

Good Easter

The eminent local historian Philip Dickinson writes, 'Good Easter, one might say, is very "Essex" in appearance and its distinctive wooden tower and spire, though modern, rising from within the west end of the nave, is reminiscent of many others in the county where building stone is nonexistent and wood and flint form the only alternatives'. That church of St. Andrew was the subject of a dreadful fire on 22nd March 1885 which destroyed both the old tower and the nave. From Philip Dickinson we also get the explanation of why the south doorway of a parish church so often has a porch. At Good Easter it was added in the 15th century. In those days the first part of the marriage service was performed outside the church, including the giving of the ring in the presence of witnesses – a legal necessity before written confirmation in the church register was introduced, and hundreds of years before 'marriage lines' or certificates were introduced. The porch kept the happy couple dry for this part of the service and the seats so often seen in such porches were provided for those witnesses, where they could see and be seen.

Many timber-framed houses, and at least eight moated homestead sites still grace the gently rolling landscape. That it was farmed in Saxon times is evident from its name, which can be loosely translated as 'Godiva's sheepfold'. Godiva, widow of a Saxon Earl, living long before the Norman conquest, bequeathed all her land to the monastery at Ely.

The chancel of St. Andrew's, which survived the fire unscathed, is long and narrow, built of flint aroud 1200 and lengthened within the next 30 years. The Victorian tower and spire rise to a combined height of 109 ft. The life of the church in earlier days, so clearly described for us by Thomas Hardy, came flooding back to us at the sight on the wall of the south aisle of a bassoon some 4 ft long, played in this church by Joseph Mott, well-known throughout the parish as the village postman. It was given to the church by his great nephew back in 1953 and was kept company by a flute of the same vintage. Sadly, both were stolen.

Just outside the vicarage gate there once stood the pillory. It had been brought here from the village green for its better protection. After being vandalised, it is now on display in the church.

Grays Thurrock

➤ 'Grays Thurrock, popularly referred to as Grays, is the administrative nucleus of the borough. Prefixed by the family name of its medieval lords, the town still possesses in its museum archives a copy of the 12th century Grant of Thurrock Manor by Richard Coeur de Lion to Richard de Grays.' – That is official, from the guide to the borough which has, these days, to concentrate more on the up-to-date information for its large population and its burgeoning industry than in its humble past as a collection of Thames-side villages which have lost their identity in the greater mass.

Grays had a great advantage – a long frontage to the Thames down which its fishermen sailed to the estuary and the fish-full North Sea. Crops of all kinds brought by boat and barge round the coast from East Anglia were unloaded here to feed the growing population. But most of all, in later years it was the loading-place for the bricks made in their millions from the brick earth in more than one area in Grays – bricks which built the ever-spreading London suburbs, the viaducts and bridges which carried the railways out of the capital and so killed the riverborne trade. An old photograph of the brickfield at Hogg Lane in 1910 shows a vast, un-believable sea of bricks, stacked in huge heaps, in rows which stretch away into the distance.

Little Thurrock, inextricably linked with Grays, also had its brickfields. In the digging of the clay by hand there was the time and the proximity to the earth to spot fossils. Examples can be seen in the museum within the library in Orsett Road, Grays. Those workmen also found evidence of the first human settlement here in the Old Stone Age. These primitive people would have told tales of the strange beasts whose remains they came across, the mammoth and the huge straight-tusked elephant. Fossil bones of these beasts found here in Victorian times were considered important enough to be preserved in the Natural History Museum in London.

One owner of much of that Thames-side property in the 17th century was William Palmer. He was Lord of the Manor, married twice but died childless in 1710. He left a legacy to have Palmer's School built opposite the parish church where it stayed until 1871. It continues still in Chad-well Road as Palmer's Sixth Form College. But for all his long-lived endowment, and his importance in his time, nobody knows where he was buried – no tomb, no monument, not even an entry in a burial register has been found.

Great Baddow

➤ The year 1381 was a big date in the Essex story. All to do with taxes and the non-payment thereof. The fishermen of Fobbing and other Thames-side villages had refused to pay the poll tax. Commissioner Thomas Bampton held an enquiry at Brentwood and ordered the fishermen's leaders to be arrested; but his soldiers were outnumbered by the crowd of protesters who chased him and them out of town and down the London road. Then they took out their anger on the poor jurymen who had been conscripted so reluctantly to give their verdict on the matter. Three of them had their heads cut off and stuck on long poles which the rebels carried before them through Essex rousing the peasantry to revolt.

They were summoned to a meeting in Great Baddow churchyard. Those who did not turn up, it was threatened, would have their houses burned down. Stand in that churchyard today and imagine that peace shattered by all this turmoil and shouting. Women and children saw their menfolk move off in a body down to Norsey Wood, Billericay, to do battle with the King's soldiers. By nightfall 500 Essex homes had lost their breadwinners.

How the church bells would have rung to bring those rebels together! In the days before the inventions of Edison and Marconi, church bells were the sound of music in every Essex village. They told everybody the time by heralding the services through the day and by tolling the curfew bell at night. The men who made them had a great sense of the importance of their bells to the village. They tuned them as finely as they could, and when they finished a sweet-sounding bell they liked to engrave it with their initials, like any artist proud of his work. They sometimes went further than that and left a message on the bell for those who would be ringing it centuries later.

All the bells at Baddow carry just such messages. The

treble is inscribed, 'I mean to make it understood that tho' I'm little yet I'm good'. Another bell declares, 'Whilst thus we join in cheerful sound may love and loyalty abound'. A third has the message 'To honour both of God and King our voices shall in consort ring'. The eighth bell sums it all up, 'The Founder he hath play'd his part. That shewes he's master of his art. So hang me well, & Ring me true, & I will sound your praises due. Chapman & Mears, Fecerunt 1789'.

Great Bardfield

➤ At the height of its importance it was a town with a busy market, but since its market cross, two-storeyed, was removed around 1769 you can tell it was a long time ago. Its shops stayed on to serve villages for miles around, then the age of the car took shoppers to the big towns and tourists enjoy the alternative trade here – antiques.

The old 'town hall' was built in 1859 in a style more reminiscent of a chapel, hidden now by pollarded limes which have reached the ample girth of middle age. Further along the street is the Cottage Museum opened in 1961 in a restored almshouse. In a small space a varied collection of local 'finds' and the implements of an earlier generation rub shoulders with a remarkable collection of corn dollies, examples of an art practised for pleasure, and to adorn the church at harvest time, when corn was long and straw was plentiful.

The old village green, outlined by a triangle of roads, has been entirely built upon, except for the little graveyard of the Friends' Meeting House. It must be said that the architecture, gloriously muddled in period, is just as attractive to the visitor's eye as a triangle of close-mown grass.

Bridge End, down by the Pant, or Blackwater has changed drastically over the last 20 years. Old cottages have been swept away and the opportunity has been taken to open up new, interesting vistas. Great Bardfield certainly is a place in which to walk about even as far as the old windmill, Gibraltar Mill, now a private house, and down the lane beside it to the watermill, with the cool sound of water splashing into the pool. Footpaths run on, up and down the riverbanks, inviting one to stroll just that little bit further.

Great Bentley

➤ Take a trip on the train from Colchester to Clacton and halfway there you will see a large village of some 600 houses, round a vast green no less than 40 acres in extent. There is a further cluster of buildings around the station, reflecting the expansion of the place when the railway came early in Victoria's reign. As Tendring District Council itself says, 'The green and the presence of a number of attractive surrounding buildings endow Great Bentley with a pleasant and unique character unlike any other village in Tendring District'.

For all the beauty of the spot there is the shadow of the Great Bentley Martyrs. William and Alice Munt and their daughter Rose Allin, together with Ralph Allerton preferred to practise their own simple religion, meeting in each other's houses. But that was against the law in 1557. The vicar, Thomas Tye, called for their arrest and a warrant was obtained from Lord D'Arcy at St Osyth. At two o'clock in the morning of 7th March Edmund Tyrrel, supported by the bailiff of the Tendring Hundred and two constables banged on the Munt's cottage door, in the region of the Plough Inn, but long since demolished.

Rose answered Tyrrel's questions, sticking to her religious belief. He was so angered that he wrenched the candle from her hand and, turning her wrist, burned the back of it until the onlookers heard the sinews crack. Yet Rose would not give Tyrrel the satisfaction of hearing her cry out in pain. He was furious and roughly handled her sick mother and her father as he ordered them to be taken off to Colchester Castle. Allerton, who had recanted his faith earlier, withdrew his confession and went on preaching while he slept rough, hiding in the woods. He was soon picked up and taken off to London to face the dreaded Bishop Bonner. There was no hope for them, though the Munts had to wait until 2nd August when they were taken into the castle yard at Colchester and burnt at the stake. Ralph Allerton lingered on till 18th September when he also was burned alive at Islington.

A memorial plaque on a brick pillar at the supposed site of their cottage tells the sad story.

Great Braxted

➤ Braxted Park is a mansion originally built for the D'Arcy family, but it was much rebuilt and extended to the form we see it today by Peter Du Cane and his grandson, also Peter du Cane who, by 1834 had not only altered the house considerably but also enlarged the park by adding neighbouring estates of Fabians and Pundicts. In 1833 the grandson Peter took over the rectory and its glebeland by building a new rectory in 66 acres of land.

There was just one problem, the whole village of Great Braxted stood within the shadow of the church and within the Du Cane's park. Du Cane simply offered to rehouse all the people further south at Bung Row, in new houses; they agreed, all the old houses were pulled down and the squire set about building a wall all round his park. He started it at the entrance by the Kelvedon Lodge in 1825, making it somewhere about five ft high, and worked all the way round. At the end of each year's completed work he had a stone placed in the wall carrying his initials and the year. That wall is still there today and it is no less than four and a half miles in circumference.

He had an icehouse in the park, built in the 18th century, with just a round hole for access. It was said by the locals that he offered £100 to any man who would live in it for a whole year without shaving or washing. Food, drink and tobacco were to be abundantly available. One man took him up – and was £100 richer at the end of the year. Ever after that it was known as 'The Hermit's Cave'.

Great Burstead

There are Roman remains at Blunts Walls, the burial of a Saxon king and the burning of Thomas Watts, the martyr, burned for his faith in 1555. But let us take the story on to much more recent times. On the night of 23rd–24th September 1916, Zeppelin L32 had crossed the Channel with orders to bomb London. Lieutenant Sowrey had taken off from Hornchurch aerodrome in his frail aeroplane into the black night to deter it and the rest of the Zeppelin fleet. He found the L32 and went into the attack. An eye-witness said, '. . . I saw, near the large cloud, some tiny flashes, like electric sparks, which twinkled brightly for an instant and then disappeared . . . They were, in fact, flashes from the explosions of the projectiles fired from the guns of Lieutenant Sowrey's aeroplane, which was attacking the wounded Zeppelin . . .'

The Zeppelin was soon in flames and fell slowly to earth in an appalling fireball, so bright that people 20 miles away said they could see clearly enough to read a newspaper. In two minutes it crashed down about one mile east of Great Burstead's houses, in meadows close to a barn and a pond. Police and firemen were soon on the scene, the latter using the pond for water to dowse the dying flames. No survivors were found. By four in the morning the crowd was gathering and Londoners from 25 miles away streamed in all through the day.

By mid-morning hundreds of soldiers had formed a tight circle 200 yards in radius all round the smoking remains to keep back the enormous crowd. The Zeppelin remains, 250 yards long and 25 yards wide, spread all across three meadows. The searchers recovered 28 bodies of German airmen. They were placed in the barn under a military guard. On 27th September they were buried with no publicity in a mass grave in Great Burstead churchyard. The Commander, Böcher, was afforded a separate grave. For a long time after the war wreaths were sent from Germany to be placed upon the graves. But about 25 years ago these remains were exhumed and sent with due reverence to the large German war cemetery in Wales, for the convenience of German visitors.

Great Dunmow

➤ Luckin or Lukin is a name often met with in Essex. It goes back to the days when people had but one name – their Christian name. A man called Luke had a big family, so each child had to have an extra name, to identify them more closely as of Luke's family – his kin in other words. So Lukin became their surname, and generations of that Lukin family gained fame and fortune in Essex in general and in great Dunmow in particular. One was Lionel Lukin, born here in 1742. He grew up to be a coachmaker to members of London's high society, but his sideline, almost a hobby, was in the building of lifeboats.

To test out models he came back here to his old hometown and sailed them on the pond now called Doctor's Pond. It was here, in 1785, that he first tried out his idea for the first ever self-righting lifeboat.

Sweetland's the butcher's in the Stortford Road preserves a facade which goes back at least to Victorian times, when T. Luckin appears as the proprietor in an old photograph. His widow Jane carried on the business through the last years of the century. Down Market Square, on what was called the Rood End side there is still a grocer's with 'Luckin' over the door, reminding us that Samuel Luckin was running it over 80 years ago.

In fact it is the number of small shops still trading which makes Dunmow a pleasant place to do the shopping for a change, taking in the eye-pleasing architecture at the same time. On the way down to Church End and the church of St. Mary the Virgin look for the house with the Dutch gables, the Clock House. On its pretty central, white-painted turret there is a clock which is said to be an exact replica of that which graces Dover castle.

Great Hallingbury

People often complain of the damage done to churches by the over-zealous 'restoration' of well-meaning Victorians. This church demonstrates what one Victorian did to modernise a church in the service of the Lord. 'John Archer Houblon wished to make the church sound and in every way fit for worship by his neighbours, tenants and his employees. He therefore repaired and enlarged; and in both he swept away – with a cold logic like that of a design engineer.' That is how Heather Cocks and Colin Hardie put it when writing the booklet issued in 1974 to commemorate the centenary of that drastic restoration. Houblon made the church workable for his modern age but, as with the glorious chancel arch of Roman brick, he carefully preserved the valuable architectural features.

The monuments and memorials which had accumulated in the main body of the church were taken down and placed all together in a room below the tower where all their details can still be read, whilst the pure uncluttered lines of the interior architecture can now be appreciated. As to the exterior, Mr Houblon used old material to extend the north aisle so that the enlargement matched the existing fabric. He rebuilt the spire as a replica of a former one which had been destroyed by lightning in 1738. He died in 1891, aged 88, having been a good 'squire', loving and caring for his people – the villagers. Tangible evidence is the memorial he paid for at Anvil Cross in memory of a villager struck by lightning there, and the school he paid for in 1851.

His house, Hallingbury Place, was built by his forebears on the site of the mansion in which Henry, 11th Lord Morley entertained our first Queen Elizabeth in 1561 and again in 1576.

Great Leighs

➤ Seventy years ago the peace treaty was signed to end the First World War. What hard times that war brought to men at the front and families back home. An amazing record of those days was written down in the rectory at Great Leighs. The Reverend Andrew Clark kept a diary of everything that happened in the village and to the men at the front throughout the war. His observations were so detailed that he filled no less than 92 exercise books – and stopped abruptly when the war memorial was finally agreed upon in November 1919. He left them all to the Bodleian Library, and there it gathered dust until a researcher chanced upon it some 60 years later and the world heard of how the folk of Great Leighs soldiered on through five years of hardship and grief.

His second-to-last entry runs '1st November 1919. The War Memorial Committee met at the Church and agreed to Mr. J. H. Tritton's suggestion of a Memorial Tablet in the churchyard wall (facing the road), a little to the north of the church tower. I agreed to have one of the thick pollard elms removed to make space for it.' Go over there on some sunny day and you can read it still. Spare a thought for Andrew Clark – and the young men who never came back.

But the worthy rector had a sense of humour too. He tells us of the man who came to buy horses for the army, in a car boldly marked O.H.M.S. An old lady, seeing this official car wanted to know what was up. The policeman standing guard, a bit of a wag said, 'Haven't you heard – they've just caught a German spy!' When the government horse-buyer came back to the car, surrounded by farmers, the old lady, thinking he was the spy, picked up a halfbrick and threw it at him. It missed him and hit the policeman on the side of the head!

Great Saling

➤ Why is this particular Saling Great? Because two settlements grew up here in Saxon times where the willow was abundant, their name for it was 'sealh', close to the Latin, 'salix', so Saling became the place name. But a closer definition was needed to tell the traveller exactly where he was, so the older settlement, the larger one to the south, was called Great and the newer one Little. As time went on Little Saling became more associated with its northern neighbour Great Bardfield and so was known popularly as Bardfield Saling.

Great Saling has proved its ancestry in recent times, showing that people lived here long before the Saxons. It was a Felsted schoolboy who helped to provide evidence when he made a personal archaeological excavation on Blake House Farm through the kindness of the late W. H. Harvey who, in 1938, had reported a great scatter of Roman remains in one of his fields. The schoolboy dug deeper and found a floor in situ. He filled his trenches when his work was done.

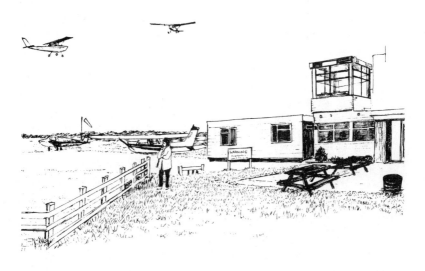

Great Saling Airfield

But man is such a busy animal that after 40 years it was dug up again, on a grand scale this time, so that all the gravel way beneath could be carted away as one of the ingredients in the new Braintree bypass. The riddle of the Roman remains only deepened when the expert archaeologists surveyed the scene in advance of the earth-movers. The skeleton of a dog was buried under the floor of the Roman building which they thought was a watermill until they found that the ditch which could have been a watercourse stopped short of the building. In the ditch they found the bones of a horse, and underneath them the skeleton of a headless chicken. The archaeologists could not make head or tail of it.

From ancient to modern – you certainly need a map to find your way to Andrews Field aerodrome just behind the village. It is worth the effort because there are welcoming signs to visitors and plane spotters, with places where they can park freely to report their presence on the edge of the apron where a flock of 50 or so light planes makes a kaleidoscope of colour against the wide, wide green of the airfield. They give the place such an air of excitement and adventure.

To the older folk in the village they bring back memories of the dark days of the Second World War, when this was the first aerodrome to be built by Americans in this country. They came in July 1942, finished the job in under one back-breaking, record-breaking year and named it after one of the famous generals in their air force, Frank M. Andrews. The hard core for the runways came from the ruins of the London blitz and the speed of construction was achieved by two shifts of men working flat out through 24 hours a day.

From it flew the Flying Fortresses, then Marauders and, towards the end of the war our own Spitfires took off to meet the challenge of the 'doodlebug' and the rocket. There are little landmarks in that history which catch the imagination, like the lump of concrete by the old main entrance in which, when it was still wet, a GI scrawled: 'Johnny Caruso, Brooklyn, New York, 24th April 1943'. Back in the village, close by the White Hart, read the inscription on the memorial, fashioned in the form of a large bird-bath in a little roadside garden with benches where the visitor can rest and wonder at the courage and the tenacity of that generation. The inscription ends:

'The warmth and generosity of the British people in this community has not been forgotten. This marker is dedicated to these friends and to our comrades who later made the ultimate sacrifice in western Europe. August 23, 1975.'

On the way back to the main road, the A120, one passes the farmhouse of Blake House Farm – one of thousands of farms throughout this land, but it stands out for a very good reason. Mr Harvey had a sense of history. He had the story of his farm traced from the 13th century onwards, and when it was all typed out he wrote an introduction: 'Being interested in the past as well as the present I decided to find out the true history of my farm and set it down as a token of my good wishes to those who may come after me.' One warms to such a man.

Great Totham

━ It is such a spreading parish with new developments along the main road, but the church and the vicarage are still isolated down a lane where in season the fields are scented with the smell of strawberries and 'pick your own' is the order of the day. At nearby Totham Hall there once lived such an eccentric man. His name was Charles Clark, born in Heybridge in 1806. His parents rented Totham Hall Farm and he moved there with them when he was 17. He was more an offspring of the muse than a son of the soil. By the time he was 19 he had written poetry of some merit.

Later he collaborated with his friend and neighbour George Johnson in writing and printing, on his own small printing press, entirely by hand, the history of Great Totham which is now so rare as to be a collector's item. As a bachelor, in older age, he became more and more eccentric. He made his poems rhyme with both the first and the last word of each line, used alliteration in titles which were as long as the poems themselves. To broadcast his ideas more widely he attached poems and thoughts to gas-filled balloons and sent them off into the blue.

He became hooked on the idea that this country was already over-populated and desperately needed the introduction of birth control. He was, in this thought, not so much eccentric as a man before his time. But perhaps he went too far in 1843 when he printed his own version of the National Anthem, parodying the original and begging Queen Victoria to stop 'her bearing tricks; On us a score she'll fix – O! save our gold . . .' But he did not have his head chopped off – he retired to Heybridge and a gentle retirement.

Great Warley

➤ It is unusual for a garden to be in the care of the Essex Naturalists' Trust, but Warley Place Gardens (in the old parish of Great Warley but now considered as Brentwood) have been overgrown and going wild for more than 50 years, and they are very special. John Evelyn, famous for his diary, lived here from 1649 to 1655. He, it is said, introduced the purple crocus to our gardens. It was Miss Ellen Wilmott, living in a much later age who put the gardens on the map.

Ellen was born in 1858 and moved with her parents and her sister to Warley Place in November 1875. Though they had a gardener Ellen was soon involved in planning the gardens, starting with a new alpine garden she designed in 1882, for which she obtained plants from specialists all over the world. She quickly mastered the art of garden design and of propagation. Alongside this interest she developed her hobby of photography and had her own book of photographs published entitled, *Warley Garden in Spring and Summer*.

By 1897 she was elected to the Narcissus Committee of the Royal Horticultural Society – a certain recognition of her growing expertise. Her parents had died by 1898, her sister had married and moved away and Ellen was left to enjoy her beloved house and garden. She had inherited no less than

£210,000, so she could spend lavishly on her gardens, employing at the height of the splendour of Warley Place 104 gardeners. Queen Mary and Princess Victoria were frequent visitors. In 1909 Edward, Prince of Wales signed her visitors' book. She dedicated the great published work of her life, *The Genus Rosa* to Queen Alexandra, so one can see what fame her gardens brought her.

From this time though Ellen slid slowly down the slippery slope of over-expenditure. By 1916 she was so much in debt she had to dismiss most of her staff. By 1918 she was managing with a skeleton staff and taking in lodgers to make ends meet. Yet, even as late as 1932 she sent out a seed list from Warley in the same old way, naming over 600 plants. She died on 26th September 1934. In May 1935 the house was sold to a man who did not live there, so the gardens were open to plunder and vandalism. The ruinous old house was demolished in 1939. In 1977 the wilderness that was Warley was leased to the Naturalists' Trust. Volunteers worked at weekends to reduce the jungle to a point where a nature trail could be formed, showing wild and rare, cultivated flora existing side by side. Permission to view the lingering remains of the glory of Warley Place can be obtained from the Trust by asking your local library for the latest address and other details.

Great Yeldham

'Patriarchal, grim and sage,
Relic of the world's dim age,
How grandly, though in iron bands,
His trunk, moss-grown and leafless stands!'

So wrote Ernest J. Bryant, back in 1931. His subject was, of course, the Yeldham Oak. Its age has defeated even the dendochronologists who count the annual rings of growth. Some say that it has seen 1,000 years of history. It stands in the middle of the village on a small triangular green, looking almost artificial now in its restraining bands of iron and its basal protection of a sloping cobbled wall. For all its necessary support it still stands as the trunk of the oldest tree in Essex, the very last example of the forest of trees which once clothed the whole valley.

It is good to see its successor growing beside it, though it is but an infant yet in terms of age. It was planted by the Great Yeldham Parish Council to commemorate the marriage of King Edward VII and Queen Alexandra on 10th March 1863.

There is a church to be enjoyed, with a big west tower and interesting architectural features for the initiated but let us close with a recommendation on refreshment by 'Yeoman' in the *Suffolk Chronicle* in 1935: 'In Great Yeldham is a hostelry whose very appearance suggests the old-world hospitality which today is rapidly becoming a thing of the past . . . The White Hart Inn the house of refreshment is called, and the very exterior appearance of this makes it a landmark to the hastening motorist . . .' That sentiment can, thankfully, be echoed today.

Greensted-juxta-Ongar

➤ In a Saxon church made of wood visitors today can claim a unique experience. This is the only such church in our country to have survived into the 20th century. Miller Christy, writing in 1888, said, 'Although it has been several times restored, it is believed to be the original structure erected as a temporary resting place for the body of St. Edmund, on its way from London to Bury St. Edmunds in 1013'. He was wrong; with the aid of the latest scientific methods of dating old timber it has been shown that St. Andrew's was built nearly 200 years before that, somewhere around the middle of the 8th century.

It is easy to imagine the Saxon settlers here, imbued with all the enthusiasm of their new-found religion, hacking down the trees to make a clearing, then using those very trunks, split down the middle and set up on others laid horizontally, to build the walls of a church which, small to us today, was a skyscraper compared with the crude huts grouped round their chief's longhouse or hall. This church has been restored and repaired through 1,100 years, that is something like 55 generations of Greensted people handing on the responsibility from one to another. One generation added the dormer windows in the 16th century and also built the brick chancel. Another, in 1848, replaced the old foundation timbers with a brick plinth, and in between the shingled spire and the tower beneath it have been added, altered and restored.

Greensted Hall, largely Victorian, stands on the same site singled out by that Saxon leader as the best place for his abode. These two buildings stand together in the fields with fine views under glorious skyscapes, still reasonably remote from Chipping Ongar and its development down through Marden Ash. It is a great place to start a walk on the Essex Way which passes by the churchyard gate.

There is a guide to be had in the church for a few pence which closes: 'Please God, St Andrews, Greensted, will ever continue a working parish and never become a turn-stiled museum'. We echo that hope.

Hadleigh

➤ 'By far the most important later medieval castle in the county', says the expert on such buildings, Nikolaus Pevsner. But it is now nothing more than the picturesque ruin of a great stone tower seen against the wide, placid waters of the Thames estuary and the low hills of Kent beyond it. It was its vast bulk which ensured the survival of these sorry remains – they were more than cowboy builders could carry away down to the time that the country became conscious of its historical heritage.

Hubert de Burgh who had virtually ruled the country during the minority of Henry III was deprived by him of all his offices in 1232. It was in 1230 that Hubert had obtained royal licence to build this castle – as much a great status symbol as a fortification, though it is possible it could have been used as an outpost guarding London from invasion up the Thames. The stone came from Kent and Surrey, brought by barge to the very foot of Castle Hill. When the railway 'navvies' were digging out the course of the line in the 19th century they came across the remains of some of these barges, already sunk twelve ft below ground level.

Poor Hubert did not enjoy the luxurious accommodation of his new castle for it was forfeited to the crown when he was tried on trumped-up charges after falling out of favour. King Henry and the three succeeding Edwards came to like Hadleigh castle very much. A governor was appointed to keep the place in readiness for the hunting parties they enjoyed in the extensive forest about it. For ten years from 1360 Edward III set in hand a thorough-going programme of repair and re-building. It did have some defensive value during the Peasants' Revolt of 1381 when it was manned by the army and sheltered some of the local gentry who feared for their lives. Eventually, as it became superfluous to royal requirements it was settled as dower on various queens down to three unfortunate wives of Henry VIII. By then it was falling into ruin again, quite neglected.

This is where Lord Rich comes on the scene, to buy it from Edward VI for £700. As Lord Chancellor he had amassed a fortune and a number of estates in Essex. He had his men cart away loads of the masonry for repair jobs elsewhere. Nature played a part in the despoliation – a landslide carried away all the buildings and the wall on the south side.

Its ruins passed on through many hands, purchasers of the land on which its stands. Dick Turpin, the early 18th century highwayman is said to have worked with a gang of smugglers which used the mouldering cellars to hide their contraband until it could be moved on to London. A century later John Constable, the great English painter captured for us on canvas the look of Hadleigh castle in its dying glory as a romantic ruin. By 1890 it was actually owned by the Salvation Army when they bought the land around it to set up a Farm Colony where men could be given basic training in agriculture to fit them for a new life in farming in the colonies.

Now its value as an historical monument has been recognised; it is maintained by the Department of the Environment within the Hadleigh Castle Country Park which is open every day, freely, to all.

Townsford Mill at Halstead

Halstead

➤ Back in 1825 Samuel Courtauld changed the town of Halstead. He bought what was then called the Town Mill from bankrupt Stephen Beuzeville. Until then it had always ground corn, first under the watchful eye of Mr. Sparrow, the miller, then by Mr. Finch. Courtauld had a new water wheel put in, not to produce flour but to drive machinery for preparing and weaving material. This innovation led to the mill up river being flooded out by backed-up water. The miller took Courtauld to court and he had to introduce a steam-driven beam engine to keep up production. The three storeys of the mill were devoted to the different processes of the manufacture of crape, so much in demand for mourning clothes. Power looms were added in a separate building in 1832.

By 1843 Courtauld's had taken on 1,000 workpeople, who spent their money in the town, so that everybody benefited from Samuel's enterprise. His employees were so appreciative of this benevolent and far-sighted man, at a time when the agricultural depression had caused so much misery and hardship, that it was said, 'Both Mr. and Mrs. Courtauld looked personally after the welfare of their workpeople, and were untiring in their efforts for the education, amusement, sustenance, and good housing of every man, woman or child whom they employed'.

Houses with the Courtauld monogram on their gables in Bocking and Halstead are still lived in by happy families. Samuel once said, 'When I die, I should like to have written on my tomb, 'He built good cottages'.' – He certainly did! No wonder, then, that 1600 workpeople got together to present him with a silver medallion at a dinner they arranged in a huge marquee in a field right next to the Courtauld family home at High Garrett in Bocking Street. It was estimated that a four-abreast crocodile of workers a mile long filed into that field to pay honour to their employer. What a sight – what a memory – it will not happen again!

It certainly will not happen again as far as Courtauld's is concerned for, as part of a great international company

95

its work in Halstead has been 'rationalised' and the white, weatherboarded, three-storeyed building we know as Townsford Mill has been given up. It now shelters within its unaltered exterior a series of shops devoted to antiques, arts, crafts, furnishings and so forth.

There are plenty of places to park a car, on the street or off it, so visitors can walk up and down the hill of the High Street and do a bit of shopping before finding their way down to the river Colne and the bridge from which that picturesque mill can be seen at the end of a pool of placid water where ducks flock to be fed. In the shadow of the mill the blacksmith's shop, once so hot and noisy in the service of the looms, is now a tea room providing lovely lunches and tempting teas. You can choose a table which looks straight out across the water to the facade of that amazing mill. A good place to refresh one's legs for the walk back to the car.

Harwich

➤ This is the port at which, from the earliest times, Kings and Queens of England have thankfully set foot on Essex soil after rough voyages across the unpredictable North Sea. Their Hanoverian connections from the 18th century onwards meant a great deal of to-ing and fro-ing in and out of Harwich. The High and Low lighthouses, now historical curiosities, were rebuilt in 1818 by the famous engineer John Rennie. At this time these lighthouses were leased out to a local family, the Rebows, who could charge all shipping using the port a set fee for this important service. When Trinity House took over the lighthouses in 1836 the Rebows were paid £159,730 in compensation, so it shows how profitable this unusual lighthouse business had been.

Yet for all this traffic and the profit it engendered, Harwich, as a port, nearly dug its own grave. It all started around 1812 when it was found that a kind of cement stone could be quarried from the cliffs, broken up, burned in a kiln, then ground to a fine powder. It was called Roman cement, 'a hydraulic cement made from calcareous nodules from the London Clay' as the dictionary explains. It had to be used as fresh as possible, mixed with sand and water to a paste which, strangely enough, would set even under water. It was such a useful invention that demand for it soared. A tremendous amount was used in the construction of the great redoubt called Landguard Fort on the other side of the harbour. Those military builders installed a mill here to crush the cement stone. They produced over 200,000 tons before leasing the mill out for commercial use.

Everybody wanted this miracle cement, including the builders putting up thousands of Regency houses in London who found it made an excellent damp-proof stucco. So the local inhabitants went on cutting away the cliffs at Harwich to get at the stone. Once this bulwark of stone was removed the soft cliffs were easily eroded by the sea, and a whole headland, where the stone breakwater is today, disappeared under the waves. At one time it seemed as if the sea might break through behind the town and cut Harwich off completely. At last the Corporation acted – digging stone at the foot of the cliffs was forbidden and sea defences were put in hand. But what really saved the town from the sea was the invention of Portland cement, which used chalk, was cheaper, and stronger. It stopped Harwich from digging its own grave!

Hatfield Peverel

➤ This large village has been by-passed these 20 years, but the main street still shows signs of its high road connections with inns, garages and cafes which constitute a kind of mini-service area. For a more peaceful part press on to the green or to the comparative isolation of the church. It needs a day of threatening thundery oppression to feel the atmosphere engendered by the witch-hunt in this village in 1566. Imagine the coercion, the torture which caused Elizabeth Francis, ignorant, uneducated, bewildered woman, to confess that she learned the art of witchcraft when she was twelve years old from her grandmother, who gave her a white-spotted cat through which her evil work was to be done, including murdering her husband and her illegitimate child. The judges at the assizes in Chelmsford genuinely believed such witchcraft could be practised, so the poor woman was sentenced to death.

The parish church of St. Andrew started out as merely the nave of the much older chapel of the Benedictine priory set up as an outlier of St. Alban's Abbey. It has been extended and restored through 500 years. When stone could not be obtained, locally-made bricks were used, as can be seen in the stair-turret and battlements of the tower. There is still a Tudor wall around the vicarage garden. Beside it stands The Priory, a private house unrelated to the old foundation. Its gateposts look impressively old, but they are an import of the present day.

A house of guaranteed 18th century lineage is Crix off the main road towards Boreham, owned by the Shaen family from 1770 to 1858, giving rise to the Shaen's shaggy dog story. Along the high road, from one of Crix's driveways to the other a great, fierce, fire-breathing, wild black dog was said to maintain a nightly patrol, offering violence only to those who first attacked it. One waggoner whose horses were frightened by this apparition, struck out at it with his whip. In a flash, man, beasts and wagon were reduced to a pile of hot, smoking ashes. Shaen's Shaggy Dog is not seen these days. Local historian T. M. Hope, writing in 1930 tells us why: 'It is rumoured that he died of spontaneous combustion at his first sight of a motor car'.

Hempstead

➤ This is not a village which advertises itself. It hides away on the B1054, seven miles due east of Saffron Walden, yet it could boast, if it cared to, of associations with two men of international repute. One was good – Dr. William Harvey, the other was Dick Turpin. What a folk-hero Dick Turpin is. We should be proud of the fact that he was a true Essex man – or should we? He did not really rob the rich of all that money to give it to the poor; most of it was spent in high-living and low dives.

He was born in Hempstead, where his parents kept the

Bell Inn. Its name was changed to the Crown and now it's known to the locals as Turpin's Tavern, offering the attraction of a very pleasant restaurant. Dick was apprenticed to a butcher in Whitechapel but soon lost the job because of his wild behaviour. He joined a gang of rustlers and butchered the cattle they stole. He tried smuggling with another gang, then moved on to burglary, even stealing from churches. By then he had a price of £100 on his head for capture dead or alive. Other criminals would not risk working with him. He moved to Epping Forest where he made a hide-out and started his career as a highwayman on the road which ran through Epping from London to Cambridge.

This was when the hero-worship began, but his glory was short-lived. He shot a man who recognised him and had to move fast to avoid arrest. He went all the way to Yorkshire, poached a pheasant there and, unrecognised, was clapped in jail. He revealed his true identity in a letter to his brother which was intercepted. So it was a sad and sorry highwayman who went to his execution on 7th April 1739.

As a boy he must have played in and around the church-yard of St. Andrew's which was built in the 15th century. But it is not as he saw it because the tower fell down on 28th January 1882, smashing the five bells and seriously damaging the rest of the church. The rebuilding of the tower was not put in hand until 1933; it was interrupted by the last war and was not completed until 1961.

Undisturbed by all the noise the long line of Harveys slept on in the family vault where up to 50 coffins have assembled. The really great man whose remains lie here was William Harvey. He qualified as a doctor when he was 24, in 1602, and went on to discover the all-important fact that the blood actually circulated continuously round the body via the heart. Not until twelve years after his initial discovery did he publish his findings, in 1628 as *De Motu Cordis*.

His reputation was such that he was appointed royal physician to Charles I. He lived to the age of 79, dying on 3rd June 1657. Though his family had by then moved from their home in Hempstead his corpse was borne to the church there with much pomp and ceremony, not in a coffin but close-wrapped in lead, and laid in the family vault. The fall of the tower made the College of Physicians concerned for the continuing safety of the great man's mortal remains. In 1883 the leaden container was moved into a specially built marble sarcophagus in the Harvey Chapel, under a bust by sculptor Edward Marshall which is arresting in its likeness to life.

Henham

➤ 'Guests, fish and news grow stale in three days time' says the author of *Strange News out of Essex, or, The Winged Serpent*, a pamphlet published in 1669. Even in those days there were people ready to capitalize on the public's gullibility, its fascination with news of a sensational nature. So a printer brought out this news, all about 'The Flying Serpent . . . which hath divers times been seen at a parish called Henham-on-the-Mount, within 4 miles of Saffron Walden'. Even the village bobby and the churchwarden said it was true.

This strange creature had a lair in Birchwood near 'The Lodge' and was first seen on 27th May 1669, when it darted out at a horseman riding by. Then two men saw the serpent as it lay sunning itself on a hillock. They reckoned it was about 9 ft long, tapering from the size of a man's thigh down to the thickness of his leg. It had piercing eyes as big as a sheep's and its teeth looked very white and sharp. They reported, also, that it had two stubby wings protruding from its back, but they appeared altogether too small to enable it to fly.

Many men, brave behind their guns, tried to shoot it, but the serpent was too quick for them, always darting back into the depths of the wood. It never did mischief to man or beast, even while it was being hunted down. Then, one day, it was gone, never to return. An expert of our own day suggests that it was no more than a large bird of the Diver family. Since the Great Northern Diver is the size of a large goose, with something of a serpentine neck it is not surprising that village gossip enlarged it out of all proportion – and it did make a good story for the newspapers of the time.

Detail of The Henham Dragon

There is not much chance of seeing a serpent in Henham today, but it is such a pretty village with its wide-spreading green, thatched-roofed cottages and a church which preserves much of its original 13th century fabric that it is certainly worth a visit. In the churchyard, south of the chancel, there is one of those graves protected by a stout iron fence anchored to a stone, going back to the early 19th century, which were introduced to defeat body-snatchers – or could it have been that there were still some people in Henham who thought the serpent might come back?

High Beach

➤ The 'Beach' in this village is hard to understand in this spelling. It probably arises from the looseness of our written language in the days when literacy was the asset of the fortunate few. A reference to the place in 1670 spells it 'Highbeach Green', but the later reference of 1734 calls it High Beech, and since it is not so far from Beech Hill Park it would seem that it was the magnificent beech trees growing here from antiquity which gave the place its name. The Epping Forest District guide shows it thus on its map but reverts to High Beach in the text where it tells us that it is:

'A true forest village ... midway between Epping and Buckhurst Hill, the only place in the District still to be as once no doubt all the villages were – settlements in forest clearings ...' It is surprising how peaceful a spot this is, considering its nearness to London and the traffic which that engenders on the M11 and the M25, and also Dick Turpin's old stamping ground the Cambridge road, later the A11, which has now been redesignated as the A104 and the B1393.

Back in the days of the first three years of Victoria's reign Alfred, Lord Tennyson lived here at Beech House, which was rebuilt in 1850. In those three years his engagement to Emily Sellwood was begun and then broken off. He also invested money in a scheme introduced by Dr. Allen, owner of the asylum where the poet John Clare was sent in 1837, to carve wood by machinery. It failed, so Tennyson's recollections of High Beech, where he lost love and money were not happy. Yet he does show enjoyment of the rural peace of High Beech in his long poem *In Memoriam* where he refers to 'the single church below the hill' which was Waltham Abbey as he heard its bell from here in the forest.

> 'The time draws near the birth of Christ;
> The moon is hid, the night is still;
> The Christmas bells from hill to hill
> Answer each other in the night.
> Four voices from four hamlets round,
> From far and near, on mead and moor,
> Swell out and fail, as if a door
> Were shut between me and the sound.
> Each voice four changes on the wind,
> That now dilate and now decrease;
> Peace and goodwill, goodwill and peace,
> Peace and goodwill to all mankind.
> The time draws near the birth of Christ;
> The moon is hid, the night is still;
> A single church below the hill
> Is pealing, folded in the mist. . .'

The church at High Beech, dedicated to the Holy Innocents was rebuilt in Tennyson's lifetime, in 1873, all of stone with a tall, slender spire competing gracefully with the trees growing all about. It was endowed with no less than 13 bells – what would Tennyson have made of that, I wonder? Today those bells are still played every Sunday to welcome worshippers, and it only requires one person – for a carillon was installed which is operated by a series of levers. The building itself is a good example of the work of the celebrated architect Sir Arthur Blomfield in what is now known as the 'Gothic Revival' style.

High Easter

The first question that will be asked about this place is how on earth it got its name. Easter is a modern rendering of the Old English word for a sheepfold. 'High' denoted the relatively higher situation of the village in comparison with neighbouring Good Easter, which itself remembers the noble Saxon Godiva who owned much of the land before the Conquest. Even today it is easy to imagine this gently rolling landscape vibrating with the bleating of thousands of sheep. Their milk and cheese and the cloth from their wool put Essex on the map of medieval Europe.

A nostalgic journey can be made down the narrow lane across from the King William the Fourth at Leaden Roding. It is a scenic journey across the bridge over the diminutive river Can by Lower House Farm and on up the hill past the unusual round house built on the foundations of the old post mill, to the village street and the beautiful old houses dotted about so picturesquely. For instance the church with its lofty tower and prominent stair turret is approached between two timber-framed, gabled houses at least 500 years old. One is the Punch Bowl now, a restaurant with a reputation, and the other is still called the Old Post Office by the locals.

Round the corner is the village shop. For nearly 50 years Derek Bircher lived there, running the shop, first with his parents, then with his brother. And in the evenings when the shop was at last closed and the stock replenished and all made tidy for the next day, Derek took up his pen and wrote the history of this village, called, *One Village in History; being an account of the history of High Easter in Essex*. It is a thorough-going history of the place as well as the story of the life of people through the ages. Derek has retired but his book is still in demand.

New houses have been built where once the blacksmith Christopher Coe helped his father fit the iron rims to cart-wheels on the tyring table laid down in the yard just outside the forge. He carried on that forge for 43 years down to 1949. Then one day he fell ill, left his hammer on the anvil and never went back. His son Eric, pursuing his own career, did not have the heart to move a thing, so the forge stood there with every tool exactly as his father had left it, even to the ashes in the hearth, until 1972 when he offered the forge and all its contents to the Chelmsford and Essex Museum. The Museum could not afford to dismantle the forge itself and re-erect it, but every movable object was collected, catalogued and labelled against the day that it can be put on permanent exhibition as a reminder of that craftsman who has dis-appeared – the village blacksmith.

High Roding

➤ Be warned, the church has to be kept locked due to vandalism. There are directions for obtaining the key. It seems strange that people will travel all the way down the blind lane from the B184, the long straight Roman road, just to commit wanton damage to an isolated, ancient place of worship, but that is the age in which we live. It is a homely enough little village church, with a very attractive Jacobean pulpit rising gracefully like a flower from a central stem. Almost hidden from view, on the floor near the vestry is a brass, nearly 400 years old, with an interesting inscription:

'John Jocelyn, esquire, interred here doth lie,
Sir Thomas Jocelyn's third son of worthy memory.
Thrice noble was this gentleman by birth, by learning great,

By single chast and godly life, he won in heaven a seate;
He the year one thousand and five hundred twentynine
   was born,
Not twenty yeares old him Cambridge did with two
   degrees adorn.
King's College him a fellow chose, in anno forty-nine,
In learning tryde whereto he did his mind alwaies
   incline,
But others took the praise and fame of his deserving
   wit,
And his inventions as their own, to printing did commit.
One thousand six hundred and three it grieves all to
   remember,
He left this life (poor's daily friend), the twentyeighth
   December.'

The seventh and eighth lines make one wonder whether he might not be another candidate in the popular pastime of finding new authors to crown with Shakespeare's laurels.

The church lost its graceful spire when it was burned down by lightning in 1832. High Rodingbury, just below the church, shows in its name element, 'bury', that it was the old manor house site of Saxon times. Inside its moat a beautiful house still stands there, but it was John Jocelyn's father, Sir Thomas, who moved the centre of administration of the manor when he built New Hall on the bank of the Roding away to the west, in the middle of the 16th century.

Highwood

It started out as just a hamlet of Writtle, then it was made a separate ecclesiastical district in 1875 and a civil parish in 1954, having been known long before as Highwood Quarter. Its church had been built as early as 1842 because it was so far for folk to trudge to Writtle, especially in wintry weather. St. Paul's is built in warm red brick with a brick-arched bellcote showing its one bell to the world and the weather. That bell was originally cast in 1654 by J. Hodson, but after developing a crack it was melted and recast in 1921, then stamped with the original initials and date! Inside, it has been sympathetically modernised, made light and airy, with plain glass windows, except the east window which is a memorial in stained glass to Robert Poole Barlow who died in 1892.

There are new houses in the street which straggles from the church down to Ward's Farm, but, in the main, they are interspersed with the old houses and bungalows – and the village hall.

Past Ward's Farm a left turn down Ingatestone road leads to early moated sites of habitation like Gorrell's Farm and Awes Farm, reminding us that John Gurel and the Hawys family were living here in the early 14th century. It passes Highwood Cottages and Budd's Farm, where Robert Bode lived in 1327, and climbs in the zig-zag turns of a narrow lane as it enters the remains of those woods which gave the settlement its name.

A walk through the wood brings one to the remains of the ancient hermitage, marked on today's maps as Bedeman's Berg, which can be translated as 'The hill of the man of prayer'. When we knocked at the door of the old farmhouse of Monk's and Barrow's Farm to ask permission to go round the house to look at what is left of that ancient hermitage we were not only given the freedom of the place but were also told about the holy well from which the owner still drew her water for family as well as livestock.

One portion of a wall is all that is left standing of the hermitage. A bush had burst through the foundation of this corner of the wall and had toppled the flint masonry into a great bed of nettles. It is not surprising that so little is left when we read the history book: '. . . it was a hermitage in the midst of a wood, called Highwood Quarter . . . It was founded by Robert, a monk, in the time of King Stephen: on which occasion the King not only granted him the ground necessary, but also whatever wood he might want for the building. He likewise gave him a pasture for cattle, and greatly assisted him in the undertaking. From Robert it went to the abbot and monks of St John's at Colchester, . . . on the abolition of monastic institutions it came to the crown, and was granted to Robert Tyrwhit, Esq, who sold it to Philip

Lantall, of whom it was afterwards purchased by Sir William Petre.'

As far as we know the Petre family still owns it and Monk's and Barrow's Farm, which got its name from the 'Monk at the Barrow (or Hill)'.

Hornchurch

➤ It started out as a village in Essex very handy to the capital for horseback commuters. It ended up in 1965 as part of the London borough of Havering. So most of its story is of its Essex past. That includes the church of St. Andrew with its 120 ft high copper-covered spire. Inside one can find the memorial to Thomas Witherings, organiser, or we might say, father of the present post office. As early as 1633 he brought order from chaos in the foreign mail service and was the 'inventor' of the registered letter service. Outside the church displays a bull's head over the east window with a fine pair of horns. It was this unusual decoration, in place of a cross, from the time of its first establishment back in Saxon times that gave the place its name – the Horned Church. It is worth a walk round, just to savour the atmosphere of the church and what it has meant to generations of worshippers.

You cannot walk round the famous old aerodrome in quite the same manner. It is an estate now of houses, shops, and schools. Happy families now grow up in comfortable homes crowding the space where pilots sat outside their huts or sprawled upon the grass waiting for the call to 'scramble!' And when that special telephone rang from Fighter Control they were airborne in minutes through the combined work of riggers, armourers, mechanics and all the back-up services needed to challenge the menace of hundreds of German bombers.

For a month, from 12th August 1940, the Hornchurch fighter squadrons were on continuous alert. They destroyed 164 enemy aircraft and many of our own young men gave their lives in our defence. The aerodrome itself was attacked no less than 23 times during the war. It is hard to believe that, back in 1916, from the same patch of grass, 2nd Lieutenant

Ingatestone Church

Sowrey took off in his primitive canvas and string aeroplane one dark night in September to seek out and destroy the great Zeppelin which he shot down near Billericay.

In 1962 the RAF gave up Hornchurch for good and it was 'developed'. But the old station badge is safely kept by Havering Council – a small symbol of a great fight for freedom.

Ingatestone

➤ A foreigner, getting on the train at Liverpool Street asked, 'Pliz, dis train, he stop at Inker-testonny?' It took a little while to realise that he meant Ingatestone! – and that was a name invented by foreigners. For that is what the Saxons were as they poured into this undefended country back in the 5th and 6th centuries. They pushed out a tribe which had been living here – a tribe of Ancient British people which had marked the place where two forest tracks crossed with a huge stone, a conglomerate called Pudding Stone brought down here at the foot of a glacier in the ice age. The Saxon tribe, or 'ing' settled here at the 'stone' and the travellers, the pioneers going on through to further lands called this place 'Ing-at-stone' – and so it has been ever since.

This is a pleasant large village with a Hall of Tudor origin, and a church which has a chapel for the resting place of many members of the Petre family which came up from Devon to build the Hall over ten years from 1539. Old cottages have been demolished so that the handsome brick tower of the church can be appreciated from the main street.

This was a much busier street when it was the main road from London to the east coast. Coaches and travellers brought much trade, so shops and inns grew up to take advantage of it.

Take just one of those inns, the Star. Its building was put up in 1480 and 'modernised' in 1643. John Walker's survey for Sir William Petre, Lord of the Manor, made in 1602 includes 'Braynwoods' which was changed into Bramwoods when Anthony Sturgeon, a Chelmsford woollen draper sold it to Jane Aylett. By 1749 it was being leased to Edward

White the local butcher who set up his slaughterhouse here. By 1850 the premises included a butcher's and a baker's, but when the Chelmsford brewer, Walter Gray bought the building in 1883 it had been a beerhouse for nearly 20 years. Today the old baker's oven has been rediscovered and restored as an interesting reminder of the time and trades the Star has seen.

Kelvedon

➤ We roved along the banks of the Blackwater on a sunny September day and came at last to the bridge which marks the division between Feering and Kelvedon. We parked the car, and by the bridge, watched a family feeding the ducks. Such simple, innocent fun, enjoyed by children, ducks and everyone! Looking downstream we were struck by the beauty of the old mill which stands astride the stream. A lot of local people still call it Roger's Mill after the last miller to make his living here, but its older name is Easterford Mill, for, long before the bridges were built, this was the easterly of two fords which the traveller had to negotiate to come into Kelvedon.

We were lucky because this was one of the three days in the year when the mill is opened to the public, when the machinery is shown at work and when people can have tea in the garden, listen to the waterwheel and dwell on times past. That wheel stopped turning in 1929 after revolving for around 1,000 years. In the age of Elizabeth I, John Fornell was the miller. A century later miller Robert Starling was up before the court, in 1641, for damming up his mill pool to get a really good head of water and thereby flooding the road.

Twenty-five years ago Lt. Col. Yule, then living in the mill house, spent a great deal of money in trying to keep the mill itself in reasonable order, but it was a losing battle.

Then, ten years ago, Marjorie Thompson bought it. Her enthusiasm and drive were infectious. With the help of her own family and 'Friends' of the mill she was able to clear the mill-race of years of junk and tons of silt. Experts overhauled and restored the machinery – and now visitors can watch the

ponderous power of that waterwheel, its brilliant arrangement of cogs and wheels to transfer that power to the stones;
and then they can buy a bag of flour, lovingly, triumphantly,
ground at Easterford Mill.

Kirby-le-Soken

The name goes back beyond the Conquest. There are
three places which stood in what was commonly known as
the Liberty of the Sokens. This was one, Thorpe-le-Soken was
the second and Walton-on-the-Naze was the third, when it
was known as Walton-le-Soken. The Soke, a Saxon word,
signified an area which had been afforded special privileges.
One of them may have been connected with the keeping of
horses, for Horsey, which means 'Horse-island' is still part
of Kirby parish. The extra 'Island' was added to its name as
early as the 14th century. That island, and Hedge-end,
Skipper and Pewit islands form the winding waterways
which feed Hamford Water and the Walton Channel north of
Kirby.

Down by the quay the outlook in that direction is as wild
and wonderful as it was back in 1681, the date from which
the parish registers now exist. And in those records we can
read of a most unusual custom, unique to the Soken villages
and observed at least down to 1707. As a token of gratitude
for the burial service read over the corpse the vicar was
offered, or even claimed, 'the best upper garment' of the
deceased. Surely the village must have gossiped when they
saw their vicar in a coat which so recently belonged to a
villager now dead?

The quay is crumbling away these days. It was in a much
better state of repair at the end of the 18th century when,
before the railway was invented, sea carriage was the easiest
way of transporting goods. At this time many a boat came
creeping in at night carrying smugglers and the wide variety
of goods, from playing cards to coffin nails, which made
their nefarious trade so profitable.

The church of St. Michael was thoroughly restored in
1870, so thoroughly that it cloaked completely the rebuilding
of 1833.

Langford

➤ Leaning on the bridge over the Blackwater, watching the waving of the weed in the swirl of the current is as therapeutic an occupation as you can find. Occasionally the glint of scales where a shaft of sunshine strikes to the depths, or the suggestion of a shadowy form within the weed indicates the presence of a fish big enough to make an angler reach for his rod. The way it keeps its station against the current with a twitch of its fins and a flick of its tail makes one ponder on the efficiency of nature. Will man's creations ever equal that beauty of form combined with functional perfection with which nature has endowed the world after millions of years of slow but sure development?

Whatever thoughts may glide through your mind in calm contemplation of the pleasant scene you will be glad to have the bridge on which to stand. In the span of history it was not so long ago that the river could only be crossed by getting your legs wet – or standing on your horse. This place got its name from the 'long ford' which Saxon travellers had to negotiate. The parish registers show how, on more than one occasion in the 18th century, the rebuilding of the bridge and its continuing maintenance were a source of worry for the village elders. It was hard on such a small place that they must provide such a long bridge at their own expense for the benefit of wayfarers who probably never spent a penny in the village.

They were already hard put to it to keep their church in repair. That church, dedicated to St. Giles, has the most unusual window seen in any church. It can be seen on the side away from the road. It is a window into the fabric of the church itself, showing how, deep under the present stuccoed surface there can be seen a section of the original, Norman fabric. When it was built some 1,100 years ago the church had semicircular ends – 'apses', which served as chapels or as the chancel. Repair and rebuilding through the centuries has left St. Giles with just the one apse – at the west end. It is the only church in the country with such a feature. That is the reason for the little window. A notice beside it explains: 'This western apse is a unique feature of the Norman period. Above is a specimen of the original masonry'. The last thorough restoration was in 1882 when the new spire and bell-turret crowned what was in essence a rebuilding.

Langham

➤ The Langham Flower Festival in the church of St. Mary is an event which adds a real bonus of perfumed pleasure to an expedition into 'Constable Country'. It is, of course, a time when the church can be opened to allcomers and there are 'friends' on hand to explain the story. For this has been a holy site since Saxon times, though this church was not built until the 12th century. A disastrous fire in 1879 and Victorian 'restoration' before and after it, meant the loss of some of its older fabric and memorials. Through it all the Vigerous family's eternal rest under the centre aisle since 1629 has remained undisturbed. Another local family with an unusual name is the Darlings, living at Langham Hall in the last century. Their memorial is the windows of the south aisle. The oldest feature in the church today must be the dug-out chest, hollowed out from a trunk of oak. You can see it in a recess of the south wall of the aisle. It is most likely that it was made to receive the money collected for the crusade, in accordance with the decree of 1166.

Walk about the place and be conscious as you do that John Constable enjoyed these woods and fields beside the Stour so much that he made them the subject of several paintings. The main road to the east, the A12, was routed carefully to preserve this area of outstanding beauty. The old main road ran up the steep Gun Hill in the days when horses hauled such heavy loads that a special notice, cast in iron and painted was set up at the bottom.

> THE DUMB ANIMALS HUMBLE PETITION
> Rest, Drivers, rest on this steep hill,
> Dumb Beasts pray use with all good will.
> Goad not, scourge not, with thonged whips,
> Let not one curse escape your lips.
> God sees and hears.

It was George Dummer, an inhabitant of this parish who found and nurtured the apple tree which is now grown internationally as Discovery.

Leigh-on-Sea

➤ It is hard to divine in the maze of roads and railway, bridges and Broadway, sports and shopping centres, the old Leigh which H. Lewis Jones looked at in 1892 when he spoke of a foreground of fishing bawleys, a line of straggling cottages along Leigh creek, backed by others rising in tiers irregularly above each other to the grand old church at the top of the hill.

In those days nearly all the inhabitants were connected with shrimping, from making the boats, sailing them, dredging up the shrimps, boiling them, packing them and selling them. The boats, called bawleys, were specially built to draw no more than six ft of water, though they weighed 20 tons and carried a big spread of sail. They all went off in the morning mist like great ghostly birds, ready to shoot their trawls as soon as they reached the shrimping grounds. In the evening they would come back up the estuary on the flood tide, all crowding together in a great mass, sometimes going aground in the shallows until the rising tide took them off again.

The shrimpers did not mind because they carried big coppers on board and boiled the shrimps on the way back to port. At the quayside in those days Lewis Jones remembered buying a delicious tea – shrimps and water cress, bread and butter, and a pot of tea – all for ninepence a head; less than fourpence today! Down by the Peter Boat pub, so called because St. Peter is the patron saint of fishermen, you can still see the boats come in and buy yourself a tasty tub of shellfish – but don't think of comparing prices!

There is no trace left of the old shipyard where, in the days of the fighting wooden walls of England, the king's ships were built, but the dedicated pedestrian can find interesting walks where old inns and unusual houses are reminders of that past, and of later days when Leigh's smugglers challenged the revenue men in their own miniature sea battles.

Little Baddow

The church is open to visitors on Saturday afternoons in the summer. Its situation halfway down the hill, just off the lane and under a spreading tree is most inviting. Six hundred years ago a man and a woman, important in the community were respectfully interred here. Not only do their tomb chests stand there still, but on them, carved life-size in wood lie their effigies. Few of these wooden effigies have survived so Little Baddow is a place of pilgrimage. Some 500 years ago an artist stood on primitive scaffolding within the church and painted the walls in glowing colours with pictures and texts from the holy scriptures.

Time passed, beliefs changed. All that is left of that artists's pious work in the name of his Lord is part of the painting of St. Christopher bearing the infant Jesus across the water. It was saved to our eyes through being covered up for centuries with layers of plaster and lime which were scraped away so patiently in 1920. Other features like the Mildmay monument of 1639 make time pass all too quickly.

On up the road is the General's Arms with its big bay windows either side of the front door and a sign which evokes the memory of Major General William Goodday Strutt, brother of the first Lord Rayleigh. Born in 1762 he became an ensign in the 51st Regiment when he was just 16. He was a brigadier by the time he was 33 and was still on very active service on 8th January 1796, when he was severely injured by a musket ball. That ball is still on view in the other family home, Terling Place, labelled, 'The Ball that Shattered my Leg'. He died at Tofts, in the village, full of age and honour in 1848.

For walkers the places in this parish must either be the banks of the Chelmer below the church or the 80 acres of Blakes Wood above it. The National Trust owns the wood but is glad of the help afforded by the Essex Naturalists Trust in its management. That body also receives the assistance of members of the RSPB. It is such an old wood that nobody knows now who Blake was. A walk through it is an escape from the rush of modern life, but do not expect it to be so peaceful at bluebell time!

Little Dunmow

The church here is such a strange-looking building. The body is like a barn with buttresses and windows of beautiful tracery. Beside it stands the campanile, what Nikolaus Pevsner, the architectural expert calls, 'a silly turret'. It was built of brick by James Brown a Braintree builder in 1872. I find it heartening to think that a church founded in 1104 as part of the priory should still be under repair and further embellishment nearly 900 years later. It has to be kept locked these days, but a notice on the door directs visitors to a house just across the road and it really is an experience to get that key and stand alone in this simple church of St. Mary the Virgin.

Because the villagers were allowed to use the Augustinian priory chapel from time immemorial that part of the priory was preserved to them at the Dissolution of the Monasteries.

The chair used for the Dunmow Flitch ceremony

One of the most touching sights in the church today is the memorial to villagers who fell in the First World War. Beautiful decoration was carried out in plaster which, through the years has crumbled so much that half the design is missing, but you will see fresh flowers placed upon it. Those 'village Hampdens' still are not forgotten. Look at the chair in the chancel. Obviously knocked up from secondhand ecclesiastical timber dated to the 13th century it is said to be one of the original chairs in which winners of the famous Dunmow Flitch ceremony were carried shoulder-high round the village. The flitch was originally given by the priory here; only in modern times did the enactment of the ceremony move over to Great Dunmow.

Little Easton

This is such a peaceful place, in the words of the Uttlesford District Council's 'Village Policy Statement' – '. . . a small dispersed village located on the west side of the Chelmer valley to the north west of Great Dunmow . . . on undulating land moulded by the river Chelmer and its tributaries . . .' With the river close by and a lot of good hedgerows this is a pleasant place in which to walk about. You may, like us, get a chance to add to your own garden from the plants on sale at garden gates as you stroll down Duck Street where most of the old houses gather, with some more modern in-filling.

But do not look for a post office or shops, they closed long since, and the local motorist has to go to Dunmow, three miles away, for servicing. The visitor can, however, find refreshment at the Stag before walking via Manor Road down the path to the church, St. Mary's. This is the place to see monuments, particularly to the Maynard family, from 1610 down to the graceful bust of Frances, born a Maynard who married Lord Brooke and became Countess of Warwick.

Her father died when she was three years old, in 1864, and, very unusually, she was made heir to his estate. Family feeling over this was so bitter that when her widowed mother moved into the family home of Easton Lodge she and her baby sister were given a bodyguard to prevent them being kidnapped. In a life of glittering nobility, which she describes in her autobiography, *Life's Ebb and Flow*, published in 1929, she was inspected by Queen Victoria as a possible wife for her youngest son, actually married Lord Brooke who inherited the Earldom of Warwick, became mistress of the Prince of Wales, then took up the socialist cause.

She still entertained on the grand scale at Easton Lodge while slipping into grave debt. In desperation she arranged to publish the Prince's love letters to her, then, saying she had received an offer of £100,000 from a publisher, she asked for that sum from King George V, through an emissary, upon receipt of which she would give him all the letters. The Royal lawyers obtained a court order, the letters were destroyed in their envelopes forthwith. 'Darling Daisy' as the Prince called her had her debts paid and no more was said. She lived on in her tottering mansion until 1938 when she died, aged 77. The old house was burned down around 1946 and subsequently demolished.

For another side of the character of this remarkable lady look in the churchyard for the tombstone inscribed:

'In affectionate memory of John Coote. Died January 16th, 1900, aged 74 years. This stone is erected by Frances Evelyn, Countess of Warwick, in grateful remembrance of long and faithful service.'

Loughton

➤ Loughton has lots to recommend it. For one thing it is close to all the delights of the capital, and suffers for that advantage in that it is very much developed, with all the roads, railways and public and industrial buildings which that entails. It is one of those modern buildings which has found a niche in the hall of architectural history. The Bank of England printing works was built in 1956 with a vast, curved, vaulted roof. Another building which stands out, midway in the High Road, probably the best-loved building in Loughton, and much visited because it is the community centre of the place, is Lopping Hall. To explain its name and the reason for its being built in 1884 we must tell a story.

In the second half of the 19th century great tracts of the old forest of Epping were literally being stolen by local land-owners who extended their boundaries, then sold off the land to developers. In 1865 the Lord of the Manor of Lough-ton enclosed 1,316 acres of the forest, put a high fence all round it and started the wholesale felling of the trees to make roads for proposed new housing estates. Just one man stood in his way. He was Thomas Willingale, an ordinary working man with no knowledge of the law. He insisted that he had the ancient right to go into the forest in winter months and lop off the lower branches of trees for fuel. He made a humble living from it.

His sons and his neighbours supported him. They climbed that fence and lopped the trees, and got seven days hard labour for their pains. One of the magistrates was himself engaged in obtaining forest land for development! But Thomas persisted, won sympathy and support from people of influence and wealth who helped him take his case to the Master of the Rolls. The poor old chap died before the case was settled, but it was his dogged refusal to give up his right to wander in the forest which caught the imagination of the nation, stopped the further development and decimation of the forest and ended up with Queen Victoria travelling to Epping forest on 6th May 1882 to declare it an open public space forever. It was the City of London which stepped in with the cash to buy out all the other interests, paying £250,000. It not only compensated the lords it also remembered the loppers, and the money paid for the extinction of their acknowledged rights was used to build Lopping Hall.

Maldon

➤ Maldon is a must for people who like to potter about where there are small boats and peaceful waters, shops rather than hypermarkets, streets rather than throughways and flyovers. Its history is there to be seen. First look at the

OS map south east of the town and you will see the crossed swords symbol which denotes the site of a famous battle; against it is written 'Maldon, 991'.

It is not a battle found in the general history books, but it certainly meant a lot to the local Saxons. The Vikings had come up the river Blackwater on a raiding expedition and had camped on Northey Island. They were a wild bunch who stopped at nothing to gain their booty. They had to be stopped. The Saxons made a terrible mistake, they let the Vikings cross the causeway from the island at low tide and form up on the mainland, when they should have picked them off one at a time on the narrow crossing. The Saxons lost the battle – and most of their finest warriors. But they fought so bravely that minstrels in the Halls of Saxon chiefs for miles around sang a song about it. This song is claimed as one of the first poems in our developing English language. Just two lines, losing much of their emotion in the necessary translation, show how the Saxon chief tried to inspire his men in the thick of the battle:

'Courage shall the harder be, heart the keener,
Mind shall be more as our might grows less.'

In the town there are three churches to prove the age and importance of this old port. One of them, St. Peter's, was ruinous as early as 1665. Against its 15th century tower Dr. Thomas Plume, born here in 1630, had a school built from the ruins of the nave. Over it he had a library room built, to which he left, in his will, all his books and pictures, with a bequest to ensure their upkeep. Climb up the winding stone stairway, enter the door and you step into the 17th century. All the books are bound in leather, placed on wooden presses or in great wooden chests, the polished floorboards are covered with rush matting. A place of great peace and atmosphere of scholarship. This is indeed one of Maldon's hidden assets.

On the ground floor, where Plume's school began, is the county branch library. Here one can look up other details of Maldon, ancient and modern, including the oft-repeated tale of Edward Bright who weighed more than 42 stone. He died at the age of 29 and needed a coffin 6ft 7ins long, 3ft 6ins wide and 3ft deep. The burial register of the church of All Saints gives the full details.

From the bridge at the bottom of Market Hill there is a pleasant walk with riverside views down to the quay beside the Queen's Head where there are several barges moored. Their great masts, their red sails and their complicated rigging are a challenge to photographers. The Queen's Head is an intriguing public house, dating way back beyond the existing deeds which date from 1700. Its bars are crammed with photographs, paintings and drawings of anything and everything to do with ships and things. It is like a museum in itself, but the official museums are the Maritime Museum nearby and the Maldon Museum in the High Street next to the Swan. Having seen the history, there is a lovely walk all along the promenade to reach, at the far end, solitude and a satisfying view of the tide sweeping in over the saltings through a hundred meandering creeks.

Manningtree

➤ What an important port this was on the south bank of the Stour in the days before the railway, when the river was navigable all the way up to Sudbury. Barges brought a golden flood of barley which was poured into the vast maltings, then the system was reversed and the malt went out to breweries and manufacturers all over East Anglia. After much demolition a new, clean Manningtree offers homes to people taking up jobs in the light industries now being developed. Few of these modern, educated townspeople would have any time at all for the belief in witchcraft.

Yet Essex is renowned for its witches, for the trials and hangings and burnings of poor, ignorant and innocent old women, and one or two men, in the 16th and 17th centuries. There had been witch trials at the assizes in Chelmsford as early as 1566, but the revival, in the 1640s of the witch scare was largely due to one man, a lawyer who lived here in Manningtree, named Matthew Hopkins. He noted the growing superstition of these troubled times and saw the deep fear local people had of witchcraft. He may have believed, himself, that so-called witches could make their neighbours sicken and die, spread disease amongst cattle and sheep or simply spoil the butter in the churn. He certainly saw a good way to make a nice, fat profit out of it.

In 1644 he said he had approached Parliament and obtained a commission from them to go on a witch-hunting tour of the eastern counties. He was to be paid a set sum for each witch he found. Thus armed he found a lot of witches, torturing people to extract confessions, and thus his fee. He also extracted money from the parish authorities as a kind of tip for ridding them of witches – just like a ratcatcher!

By 1645 he had arrested 200 people and clapped them in gaol. Sixty-eight of them were hanged or burned at the stake. He even wrote a pamphlet setting out all the points in favour of his evil and underhand work. No wonder he was called 'The Witchfinder General'. Some people say that when the witchcraft scare had passed and he was denounced he retired discreetly to Manningtree, to die in his bed; others say that he was challenged, and hanged. Nobody knows.

Margaretting

➤ The parish council has been adventurous and older folk have reaped the reward. The almshouses on the corner of the London road and Maldon Road became redundant, there were no takers, and they were very old-fashioned. The council sold them for private restoration as flats and vested the money in the Margaretting Relief in Need Trust. The income is used to help old people stay in their own homes as comfortably as possible, and also provides a general service for all older folk, a minibus to take them into Ingatestone every week to collect pensions and do shopping. What a nice idea!

One very attractive feature in the centre of the village is the village sign, a representation of St. Margaret and the church, carved in wood by Harry Carter of Swaffham. It was bought with funds accruing from the Queen's Silver Jubilee celebrations and put up in April 1978 on the very brink of the village pond. That pond had been in danger of loss through neglect until Essex Conservation Volunteers cleaned it out and created the haven for water fowl it now is.

Walk the footpaths down to the church across the railway and see the reredos, carved not by famous artists, but by local men attending the wood-carving classes instructed by Charles Jennings at the building yard in Penny Lane early this century. St. Margaret's is essentially of 15th century construction with an amazing timber tower, belfry and spire. Most of the church is contemporary with it, including the north porch, also carried out in timber.

The east window shows a feature now of great rarity. In stained glass, much restored, but still impressive in its three-light 15th century composition, a 'Tree of Jesse' is depicted, showing, with appropriate figures, how Christ was descended from Jesse, the father of David.

Marks Tey

➤ Marks Tey as a village bears all the scars of suffering from its proximity to the A12. That old Roman road along which the chariots dashed straight as an arrow from London to Colchester has been widened to accommodate the juggernauts and the junction with Stane Street, the A120 to Braintree and the west. Alongside the road the railway runs where inter-city expresses pound non-stop to Norwich. Through 2,000 years Marks Tey has seen hosts of people coming and going, but very few staying. One family that did was the Marks. They held the land here by service to the mighty Mandeville. 'Tey' means an enclosure in the language of the Saxon settlers and the Marks' name was added to distinguish this village from its Great and Little neighbours. As early as the middle of the 13th century the village was also known as Tey at Elms because of the huge elm trees which grew there, particularly along the Coggeshall road.

From mighty trees of yore to the humble primrose of today. The soil and the climatic conditions in this part of the country favour the raising of plants for seed. Kelvedon Wonder is a garden pea that, after a century, is still asked for by amateur gardeners. Even before that the same folk were crowding into Colchester every year to show off their best blooms in the annual Primrose Feast. And now, in recent years, a bridge has been built back to those happy occasions by the Bypass Nurseries here at Marks Tey.

They have introduced a new and wholly professional show of flowers called the Primrose Festival which is held late in February when their plants are in full flower under glass. The Festival gives visitors the chance to see some 250,000 individual plants in a range of colours and shades which outshines the rainbow and dazzles the eye in winter gloom like the lights on a Christmas tree. For two days only is the public admitted, and the entrance fee is donated entirely to charity. That is a generous gesture for this is not a place where primrose plants are raised for sale; it is a laboratory where plants are grown to maturity and their seed harvested on behalf of plant breeders from all over the world. They send in small quantities of seed which they have developed under scientific conditions, and Bypass Nurseries, one of the last of such companies in this country, sow them, grow them and harvest the vastly increased bulk of seed which is packaged and returned to the breeders for their commercial exploitation. Bypass Nurseries keep no seed, but they do keep the secret of the parentage of the seeds they grow – primroses, salvias, cyclamen and so on. The breeders code the envelopes of original seed and from the plants raised every seed is returned to the breeders. But there is a chance on one of those open days to buy a surplus plant from that kaleidoscope of colour.

One lasting reminder of the old village life of Marks Tey is preserved in the Chelmsford and Essex Museum – it is the village pump, once the centre of news and gossip as people waited for their turn to draw water for the day. It was left high and dry on the verge of the A12, then further widening threatened its survival. Now, in the museum, it demonstrates to a modern generation one of the drawbacks of old village life all too often clouded by nostalgia.

Matching

➤ To the best of my knowledge there is only one Wedding Feast House in Essex. Yet what a generous and understanding thought lies at the bottom of it. Back in the days when dates hardly mattered and a marriage was a solemn affair celebrated in the presence of God in the parish church, half the village would be related to the bride and the groom and they all wanted to join in the celebration of such a joyous occasion. Finding a room large enough was a problem, and an expense.

A man called Chimney (and that is all that is known of him) had a row of cottages built, of which the upper storey was separate, and all-in-one with its own staircase. This was the room that he provided for those wedding feasts. Although the guide book of a 100 years ago reports it as 'ruinous', it has been most sympathetically restored and can be seen keeping the church of St. Mary company amidst oak and chestnut trees in the kind of setting for which the photographer can usually only dream.

Add to this the Hall on the other side of the lane, which is private thereafter, the water-filled moat which laps it round

Wedding Feast House, Matching

and the fine, big dovecote which once supplied the lord with his winter meat and you have what some writers might call a 'time capsule'. This is a place of perfect peace, away from all traffic, down a no-through road which passes in a right angle a lake on which hundreds of water fowl can be seen in their wild state.

Mersea Island

➤ Comes a fine day and families in Essex seem to say, 'Let's go to Mersea' – and a tailback of cars soon queues to cross the Strood, the only access to the island. The Strood has connected it directly to the mainland since it was first built by the Romans as a causeway. 'Strood' was the early name for marshy ground, originally applied to the muddy channel but somehow the name was transferred to the roadway itself.

The Romans left behind a wheel tomb, a type reasonably common in other parts of their empire but rare in this country. Its site is a private garden some 200 yards east of the church of West Mersea, discovered and excavated in 1896. It is a big affair – a circular wall 65ft in diameter and three ft thick, with internal walls radiating like spokes from a small central chamber.

The mystery of the significance of such a large construction for such a small tomb is eclipsed by the mound which gave its name to its location – Barrow Hill, on the north side of the island's central plateau. It was excavated in 1912 and found to be about 23 ft high and 110 ft round. It was a big mound to dig through, and all that was found, right at the centre was a tiny chamber 18 inches square and just a little more than that high. In that small space was a casket made of lead, and within that was a glass vessel containing the remains of the cremation of a human body. What an important person he or she must have been!

But forget the past and enjoy the present on the beach at West Mersea, or drive to the eastern end, now protected as a country park, though you will find a scattering of caravans on the seaward side of East Mersea church.

Mistley

➤ When building council houses at New Mistley in 1946 workmen found a burial urn with incinerated remains – not the only evidence of Roman life here. From very early times the place grew and prospered with its wharves on the river Stour. It owed its continuing success to Richard Rigby whose father Edward had bought the Hall in 1680. Richard inherited it, rebuilt it in a 700 acre park and had it judged by Horace Walpole as 'The charmingest place by Nature, and the most trumpery by art . . .' It was demolished in 1845. As Coller, writing in 1861 says, 'The land thus set free gave greater scope to industry – allowed commerce more elbow-room for its efforts . . .'

Richard had intended that the New Mistley which he planned and built down to the river should be more than a commercial centre with granaries, maltings and warehouses; it should be a spa, and to this end decorative features were included in the development of the place. One of them, a little square with a fountain graced by a swan can still be seen.

The rebuilding of the church in 1735 was part of Rigby's plan, but his son, also Richard, had it completely redesigned again in 1776 by the great Robert Adam, with an elegant tower at each end of the nave. That nave was pulled down when yet another church was built and the towers remain in the care of the Department of the Environment as 'classified' monuments to Mistley's magnificent past. One of the great sights today is the flock of swans, estimated at some 600, which glide with such grace along the river.

Mountnessing

➤ Mountnessing windmill was reopened by the late Hervey Benham on Sunday, 13th November 1983. It had been put in full working order under the supervision of one of the last millwrights to practise the craft, Vincent Pargeter. Essex County Council has owned the mill since 1956, when it stood as an interesting but dilapidated and deteriorating landmark just off the old A12 which, in the days before the bypass, was very busy indeed. Weekend and Bank Holiday motorists had a good view of it as they inched slowly through the village past the Prince of Wales.

That public house was, in fact, a bakery in earlier days, getting its flour straight from the mill across the road, which had been standing since 1807 at least. That was the date offered by Robert Agnis whose family ran the mill through-out its working life down to 1924, and then again for a short period in 1932–3. This was not the first mill on this site. There is evidence of a windmill on the mound as early as 1477, and Ogilby and Morgan's map of 1678 shows a mill still working there. It is approached from the main road along '. . . the chace lane from the turnpike road' as it is described in a lease of 1861. In those days the 'round house' – the brick built base through which the strong central post rose up to take the whole weight of the mill – was thatched. It made a charming picture; the white clapboard mill and sails rising above the golden thatch and the warm red brick of the perfectly circular base. Rats ruined the thatch, its replacement was uneconomic so, in 1919, it was replaced with tarred boards.

In the 1930s the poor old mill went into a decline, aggra-vated in May 1949 when it was struck by lightning, but then, when all seemed lost, the County Council took it over and it was restored to working order. A Friends of Mountnessing Mill society has been formed and volunteers show the public round their mill on publicised afternoons once a month from May into the autumn. Full details of this attractive old mill, historical and technical, can be found in the late K. G. Farries' *Essex Windmills, Millers and Millwrights*.

Navestock

Where the river Roding winds there is a little place which even had the compilers of the Domesday Book in two minds back in 1086. Navestock is one of only three places entered twice in that record as far as Essex is concerned. Its second entry is entitled 'The other Navestock' – Fyfield and Melesham (Great Leighs) are dealt with in the same manner.

That division has continued down to the present day. On the one hand Navestock Hall and the church mark the site where the Saxons first settled, cleared the land of trees and, upon conversion to Christianity, built their first primitive church of timber cut straight from the forest. A mile to the south is the 'other' Navestock where the nucleus of today's Navestock has evolved, though its problem of identity has been complicated by a third hamlet to the east being called Navestock Side. The name arose from that first settlement on the nave, or headland, where the trees were felled and the stumps, or stocks, were still to be rooted out. All the land had been vested in St. Paul's cathedral by the pious Saxon lord around AD 970.

Today, it is hard to believe that this country parish has continued farming its fields within three miles of Romford's metropolitan bustle. Two very old stones, called the Navestock Stone and the Richard Stone could once be seen in the woods at Curtis Mill Green. They marked boundaries in the days when the forest of Essex was a cohesive whole and the actual extent of Waltham forest had to be marked, for it was specially reserved to the King for hunting and other rights. The Navestock stone was the only one remaining in situ by 1905 when H. Burdon wrote: 'The stone was found sunk deep in a ditch embankment at the rear of a row of quaint cottages on the outskirts of Curtis Mill Woods . . . From this point we followed the pretty broken piece of woodland down an open glade, in which we found the Richard Stone lying prostrate . . .'

Newport

➤ 'Port' in earlier days had the basic meaning of a town, usually one with a charter for a market. So this village became a town when the market was transferred from Clavering or some neighbouring place. But it did not keep that status for long, for Saffron Walden had that market transferred to it in the same, 12th century. Many of the old houses are still standing, kept in good repair by people who work in London and commute by rail and road. Even the old prison, a good-looking building of the 18th century has been converted to superior dwellings.

There was a time in the 16th century when the Guildhall, or Town House, presented to the inhabitants by Robert Driver in 1544, stood empty with the diminution of trade. This is where Mrs Joyce Frankland comes into the picture. Having been widowed twice, her life centred round her only son. He was riding to London in 1581 when his horse threw him and he was killed. Her grief knew no bounds. One friend who came expressly to console her was the Dean of St. Paul's. He said, 'Comfort yourself, good Mistress Frankland and I will tell you how you shall have twenty good sonnes to comfort you in these your sorrows which you take for this one sonne.'

So he sowed the germ of an idea. It grew and bore fruit in 1588 when with further encouragement from friends Joyce started a school in the former Guildhall and engaged a master at £20 per annum. In 1837 that building was demolished so that a new school might be built there with room for 60 boys on the first floor. The ground floor was rented out – as a granary! The present Newport School, built in 1878, has had numerous extensions, including a Memorial Hall built in 1920 as a war memorial of Old Newportians killed in the First World War. When Saffron Walden's grammar school was closed children from that area were found places here at Newport – a kind of quid pro quo for losing their market to Saffron Walden all those years ago.

Panfield

➤ The heart of this little settlement, 'open country on the banks of the Pant' as the Saxons described it, was and still is its parish church which stands a little to the east of the later development of the village. It is mostly of a 15th century rebuilding with walls of flint and pebble rubble, but it has had to be restored through that time, as is evident from the timber-framing of its south porch.

There is a nice story here about the way in which one old inhabitant is remembered. Edward Bangs, baptised at the font here on 28th October 1591 took the dangerous passage to the new American colony and religious freedom. He prospered and his descendant, Mr. W. E. Nickerson of Boston, Massachusetts came back to his ancestor's village recently and gave ornaments for the altar and utensils for worship in his memory. Another memorial is the church clock, it celebrates Queen Victoria's Golden Jubilee in 1897.

Panfield Hall lies to the south of the church. Its oldest part, on the west side, dates from 1546 and its original building. The eastern part was completed in 1583. It looks a handsome place in a peaceful landscape.

One man who lived in the rectory here for 26 years in the latter half of the 17th century was John Ouseley. He was a pioneer in the collection of historical information about Essex. It was his collected papers, which never reached print themselves, that were such a terrific help to later historians, like the great Philip Morant, and they were not slow to acknowledge their debt. Yet the Reverend John Ouseley was such a humble and unassuming man that nothing is now known of his own, personal history.

Pleshey

Pleshey owes its name to the Normans. This is a place which, all in one spot, shows evidence of occupation by the Ancient British, Romans, Saxons and Normans. At one time it was called Tumblestown because of all the old entrenchments, mounds, ditches and tumuli which each wave of settlers had raised or dug to defend themselves or bury their dead. The Normans called it Pleshey because, in their old French language that meant a fortification made by growing a thick hedge, preferably a prickly blackthorn, and bending it back on itself by interlacing the branches.

This is a place which, since its mention in Shakespeare, has been fully covered in the history books and the tourist literature, but one thing has been left out. Pleshey is the home of the Darby Steam Digger. Thomas Churchman

Darby, a farmer here, was of a mechanical turn of mind. In 1877 he planned a steam-driven machine which would turn the rotary motion of the engine into a heavy digging action out in the field. This was at a time when foreign competition made it vital for English farmers to bring their prices down, and Darby saw that some automation could be the answer.

The prototype of his machine was, in fact, too ingenious. It actually 'walked' along, digging as it went, but when its cast-iron components came up against stones in the soil they shattered like glass. Darby persevered, he had his digger made in steel and showed it at the Royal Agricultural Show in 1880 where it won a prize. But farmers were so very conservative, they could not envisage ploughing without the plodding horse, and so the digger was not a commercial success, though around Pleshey, where people saw it in action, you could see seven of them at work.

Now everything on the farm is mechanised, automated, computerised, but the Darby Digger has gone. There is not one working part left in the world to be a monument to that remarkable man, so much in advance of his time.

Purleigh

➤ What place in Essex can connect England with America and Russia in one short span of years? It is Purleigh, ten miles south east of Chelmsford.

The Americans paid for the restoration of the 13th century tower of All Saints' church in 1892 because Lawrence Washington, who had been rector here from 1632 to 1643, was great-grandfather of their first President.

The Russians invaded in 1897. A group of them, including some English sympathisers, came from Croydon to found a colony of brotherhood here, living simple lives of self-sufficiency on 16 acres either side of the lane from Cock Clarks to Cold Norton. They trod their own clay, made their own bricks and built their own houses. The first of them is now known as Grey House and another is called Colony House to this very day. They tilled their fields, gathered their crops, and all seemed sweetness and light for the 80-

Colony House at Purleigh

odd anarchists. But within a couple of years they had fallen out among themselves, disbanded their brotherhood and gone their separate ways. Only those strongly built houses stand as their memorial.

Rayne

This village for years has been divided by a stream, a river of traffic pouring along the A120 as it heads from Harwich and Felixstowe to the motorways 1, 11 and 25, to London, the west and the north. The Braintree bypass will shortly ease that burden as it exits on to the A120 west of Rayne.

The focal point of the place today is the church. Before it

was rebuilt, in 1840, it gave rise to a proverb. 'It won't be long before you're saying your prayers at Rayne'. This goes way back to the time of Edward III in the 14th century when the wife of the Lord of the Manor, John de Naylinhurst, was having a terrible time in labour. Some of her attendants went to the church, to the altar erected to the worship of the Virgin Mary in the south aisle and prayed for their lady in her hour of need. They were astonished when they saw the statue of the Virgin smile in answer to their prayers. They just knew that her ladyship was safely delivered. They flew back to the house to be met with the good news from the other servants. For many years after that expectant women made their way to the church to pray for a successful pregnancy and a prompt delivery.

After being closed for six years from 1834 the church was rebuilt, but the strong Tudor brick tower was, thankfully, retained and restored. It gives the church such a sturdy, strong personality. In a glass case under that tower can be seen a knight's helm. It is only a replica. The story is told in *A View into Essex*: 'Sir Giles Capell, Lord of the Manor, was one of the Knights led by Henry VIII who challenged all comers from the continent for thirty days at the Field of the Cloth of Gold in 1520. In his will he wrote: 'I will that my beste helmett and my armying Sworde be sett over my funeralls according to the devise of the harrauld.' They remained in position over his tomb in the church until the 1840 restoration, when the Capell tombs were unaccountably destroyed and the armour was removed by the builder. The helm was sold to Miss Courtauld for ten shillings and she gave it to a friend who sold it for a great sum to an American. It is now one of the prized exhibits of the Metropolitan Museum of Art in New York.'

Rettendon

➤ The parish of Rettendon is strangely shaped like the head of an alsatian with its nose pointing to Hanningfield reservoir. A journey round it offers many points of interest. The Bell inn has quietly gone on giving rest and refreshment to travellers on the busy road, the A130, for close on 200 years. The village has been much extended as we can see from the fact that Curds Farm, now in amongst the recent houses and bungalows has actually been given a street number. Past Buckhatch Farm there is a private road to Hyde Hall, on the site of a house which was here as early as 1412 when it was called Le Hide. The gardens are open to the public on certain summer days – and they are interesting enough to have been featured on television.

'Mill House' on a gate – and a green mound behind the house are the last reminders of Rettendon windmill. That was a mill which was bewitched if ever there was one. There was a mill here before 1678, then a new one was built in 1797 – and its sails swept so low that three-year-old Elizabeth Jefferies, wandering near them, was struck and fatally wounded. In 1853 the miller's 24-year-old son, George Borrodell risked pushing a wheelbarrow past the mill as the sails were turning; he was caught by the downward swish of a sail, and lived but five hours. In the 1860s William Myhill had set himself up here as miller, baker and brickmaker.

William Marsh was the last miller and baker. On 3rd January 1873 that evil spirit struck again – the mill caught fire and was burned down, despite the valiant efforts of the horsedrawn fire engine summoned from Chelmsford.

Rettendon Hall recalls memories of the Humfreys, who lived here from 1605 to 1727. The line ended with bachelor Edmund Humfrey. He it was who arranged for his own splendid monument which spans the breadth of the north aisle of the church. He reclines, in effigy, on a pedestal, pointing heavenwards with his left hand. Other figures crowd round him in fascinating costume of the 17th century.

Rivenhall

➤ The story of this place has been researched back to Roman times with the archaeologists declaring, 'In a rural situation an example of the continued occupation of a villa after the historical end of Roman Britain is provided by Rivenhall. There it can be seen how two large domestic

135

buildings and an aisled barn were modified during the 4th, 5th, and 6th centuries to suit the needs of the agriculturally based estate.' When the church of St. Mary and All Saints was restored recently a Saxon window was reopened and all around the church, by its foundations, evidence of human occupation of this site continuously from Roman times has been established.

Probably the best known person to be born in this small village is Thomas Tusser who saw the light of day here in 1523. He was what might be termed the Farmers' Poet, with his *The Hundreth Good Pointes of Husbandrie* published in 1557 and revised in 1573 to no less than 500 'good points'. He was not much good at farming himself and tried various moves about the country. On his death Fuller said, 'He spread his bread with all sorts of butter, but none would stick thereon'.

Whatever his ability at farming, his poetry lives on and on; straightforward advice on farming and housekeeping written out in rhyming couplets which are very easy to remember. He goes all through the year with the jobs to be done on the farm and in the house, but at Christmas-time he relaxes a bit, saying:

'Good husband and housewife, now chiefly be glad
Things handsome to have, as they ought to be had.
They both do provide, against Christmas to come,
To welcome their neighbours, good cheer to have some.
Good bread and good drinke, a good fire in the hall,
Brawn, pudding, and souse, and good mustard withal.
Beef, mutton and pork, and good pies of the best,
Pig, veal goose and capon, and turkey well dressed,
Cheese, apples and nuts, and good carols to hear,
As then, in the country is counted good cheer.
What cost to good husband, is any of this?
Good household provision only it is . . .'

Rochford

➤ You always know where you are in Rochford – with North Street, East Street, South Street and West Street, and the Market Square in the middle it is as good as a compass to the traveller. The parish church of St. Andrew shows its age in 15th century architecture and the rebuilding of its tower in warm, red brick a century later. A church of another kind is remembered in Chapel Cottages in North Street. It was once the chapel of the Peculiar People, a religion now merged with the Union of Evangelical Churches.

It all started when James Banyard, a shoemaker in this town, went to hear a couple of evangelists putting forth their message with missionary zeal. That message caught his imagination. He was inspired to preach himself and so impressed a meeting that they continued as his own congregation and, in 1838, built their own chapel. Their name of Peculiar People referred to their tenets of belief and was taken from the Bible.

One of those tenets was their belief in healing through anointing with oil and the laying on of hands, seen by the general public as a total rejection of medical aid. The development of the National Health Service and the advance of medical research caused a compromise to be found on this issue. The general message of simple faith spread through villages both sides of the Crouch and more chapels were built, even though the congregations were of the poorest people.

A hundred years ago it would have been a regular Sunday sight as these country people, so happy in their faith, walked along to chapel together, carrying the dishes and bowls which contained their dinners. These were put on the big central stove which heated the chapel to warm up nicely while their owners spent the day in prayer and praise and preaching. With a break for dinner, of course.

Converted mill at Roxwell

Roxwell

Roxwell is just a sleepy village, on the road to nowhere, not too much developed in recent times, so there are a good many Roxwell folk, born and bred in the village, to hand down lore and legend to the new generation. One of their stories is all about the day the boiler burst.

It happened at the watermill just off the end of the village street. The wheel was turned by the rather uncertain flow of the Roxwell brook until Victorian ingenuity saw to the installation of a steam engine. From 1868, when that engine was already working, right down to 1926, the mill ground its flour under the watchful eye of John Shepherd Ray and his son Ernest. Nobody knew when the steam engine was actually installed with its massive boiler over twelve ft high and four and a half ft in diameter.

Ernest carried on with it after his father's death in 1889 and had it checked and overhauled in 1899. On February 5th 1901, very early in the morning, Ernest lit the fire beneath that boiler. By 7.15 am it had reached its operating pressure. The safety valve did not blow off to give any warning. Suddenly, with a bang, a very loud bang, the boiler exploded, and took off like a rocket. It soared into the air, striking a corner of the mill roof on the way, and landed some 60 ft away, only yards from the houses, and the people, on the village street. What a commotion! But Ernest had it all repaired and carried on for another 25 years – a brave as well as a jolly miller.

In 1950 the mill was converted to an unusual and interesting house by sandwiching the clapboard and timber-beamed construction between two thick layers of concrete. That is why doors and windows appear so irregularly – they are the original openings put in to suit the convenience of the mill.

Saffron Walden

If you want to be lost for a moment in olden times take a look at the house in Church Street which was once the Sun Inn, where Cromwell ordered his men to seek the King and bring him in for trial – and ultimate execution. You will see that the plaster on its gable above the shop window has been worked into a wonderful picture, in deep relief, of two men having a fight. One has a mighty club, formed from the axletree of a cart, with a wheel from that same cart as a shield while the other fellow seems to be equipped only with the normal sword and buckler.

What does it mean? Well, the story goes that Tom Hicka-thrift owned a meadow in which 30,000 sheep were grazed, the villagers disputed his right to that land. He would not give in to them, so they decided to turn up in a bunch and threaten him. Tom picked up his axletree and defeated the lot of them. The story grew with the telling, so the pargeter, or plasterer skilled in such ornamental work, thought it would make a very nice subject for the Sun Inn when it was redecorated in 1676. Some people say the whole scene is much more meaningful – an oblique reference to the sun god and the endless rolling of the wheel of light and darkness.

Everybody knows that this town, by its very name, was famous for the saffron crocus grown in medieval times for its gorgeous yellow dye as much as for its use in cooking. But 100 years ago it was just as famous for its hollyhocks, available in astonishing variety from the nurseries of Webb and Brand. They owed their hollyhock fame and fortunes to an ordinary person like you and me – old Charlie Baron, a shoemaker in the town. After a day bent over his last he was glad to get out in his garden where his hobby was holly-hocks. He crossed them and recrossed them until he had a bower of flowers in wonderful new shades, and semi-double too. He did it just for love of that plant. It was very fortunate that William Chater, a professional nurseryman, knew Charlie and could take over his experiments.

In 1847 he issued what was then the most comprehensive catalogue of named varieties of the hollyhock, and he re-vised it every year down to 1873 with a continuing variety of new types and colours. Then disaster struck. A terrible infection called the hollyhock disease spread throughout his nurseries and all those beautiful, new and delicate varieties sickened and died. For years not a hollyhock was to be had while new techniques of raising disease-free plants were evolved. The rare and tender plants grown under glass had to be abandoned; hardy plants were cultivated and raised from seed only.

But William Chater did triumph over his tribulation and before he died in 1885 he passed on his knowledge to Webb and Brand who could claim, in 1900, to be the largest growers of hollyhocks in the world.

St Osyth

━ Thousands of people enjoy holidays in chalets and caravans along its five-mile coastline. Actually this place was first called Chich, the Saxon word for a bend, because the first settlement here was by a bend in the creek which runs down to the Colne estuary. In later days the name became Chich St. Osyth, and now the 'Chich' is quite forgotten. So how did St. Osyth creep in? This is the story.

Osyth was the daugher of the great Frithewald, King of the East Saxons. She grew up in the Christian faith and became prioress of a nunnery founded here by her father in the tiny settlement of Chich. In the autumn of A.D. 653 a band of Danish raiders came up the creek in their boats, pulled them ashore here and went on the rampage. They broke into Osyth's nunnery intent on humiliating the nuns and subjecting them to sexual harassment, as it might be called today. Osyth stood before them, shielded them, faced up to the Danish chief. He demanded that the nuns deny their faith, she rejected his demand. He, in his wrath, ordered her to be beheaded, and one of his men immediately carried out the dreadful deed.

Osyth died for her faith and for her nuns. Legend has it that she straightaway bent down, picked up her head and carried it to the church where she struck the door with her bloodstained hand to indicate that she should be buried there. On the spot where she was beheaded a spring of the purest water flowed forth from that very moment – and the place is still known as Nun's Wood today. She was canonised, and we only think of St. Osyth as a nice place for a holiday.

Salcott

The name of this parish, meaning a salt house, is one of the clues in trying to identify the mysterious red hills, marked as such on the Ordnance Survey maps right on the coast from Clacton down to Goldhanger. The fact is, they are not very big hills, just mounds, man-made mounds, and they are about 2,500 years old. Some of them are up to 30 acres in extent, even though they rise no more than five ft above the original soil.

The soil has not been dug out and heaped: this is the accumulation of waste product left behind by early man. There are hundreds of these red hills, despite the fact that many of them have been ploughed away or overtaken by the sea. The history books are very cagey about what they were, but, putting two and two together, adding clues like the name of this village and other places in the area, the answer could be – salt. Ancient man needed salt. He collected it from the seashore, dried out from tide-forsaken pools by the summer sun. He divined that sea water could be boiled away to leave its salty deposit. That salt, the gold of the Iron Age, could be traded far inland for other vital necessities like tools, weapons and hides. So the Salcott man made big, wide, shallow pans of thick, crude pottery, put them as near the tide as he could, filled them with sea water, then lit a fire beneath them using the brushwood and timber he could gather on the foreshore. All he had to do when the water was boiled away was to scrape up the salt.

Sometimes the pans broke and their pieces were simply left lying in the growing pile of ashes. Imagine the amount of ashes and other detritus which would accumulate over 100 years of salt making in this manner. Roman pottery found in these red hills shows that the salt industry in this area was carried on down to Christian times.

Another fact about Salcott not generally known is that its church was so badly damaged in the Great Essex Earthquake of 1884 that it had to be rebuilt.

Shenfield

The name of this place should have been extinguished in 1934 when as a civil parish it was divided between Mountnessing and Brentwood, but for all its merging with the latter in its highways and its houses those 1,000 years of growing as an individual village have given it a personality that is still preserved in quieter places, especially since the bypass round Brentwood brought release from a traffic flow which by now would have been quite unbearable.

Up by the church of St. Mary the Virgin there is peace to be found in a churchyard with a difference. A past rector, long since dead, planted seedlings of specimen trees. Now they can be seen in all their adult glory – an arboretum in miniature. Tree trunks were used in the church in a most unusual way – to make an arcade of timber columns, five of them, each hewn from a whole tree, with moulded capitals and bases as would be seen in stone columns, supporting a 60 ft length of roof. They were set up in the reign of Henry VII, around 1500. Their whole situation and purpose were altered in the 1830s when a good deal of restoration was required.

The only tomb memorial in the church is that to Elizabeth Robinson, nee Merrell, who died in childbirth in 1652 when she was only 16. Part of the inscription reads 'That she might unite in a closer bond of love the families of her Father and her Husband'. This could well be a hint of different sides taken in the Civil War. Another strange division is seen in the memorial above the font to Joseph Tasker, who lived at Middleton Hall, for he was in fact an ardent Roman Catholic who provided a large part of the funds towards the building of the Roman Catholic cathedral in Brentwood. He is remembered here because he served for many years as an overseer of the poor of the parish in the days when they met in the church vestry.

Southend-on-Sea

➤ The Reverend Thomas Archer was born around 1750. He made his ecclesiastical way via curacies at Prittlewell and at Southchurch. We get a good description of the man in his prime from a contemporary who described him as one of the old school, following the fashion of an earlier day, with blue frock-coat, white corduroy breeches and grey worsted stockings without gaiters. While at Prittlewell he affected to smoke a pipe on his way to church, leaving it in a niche in the porch. He loved hunting, to the extent that he broke a rib when he fell after putting his horse to a stile in Southchurch.

He was a man of no mean literary talent too, with a penchant for versifying. He sent excellent verses into the local newspaper under the pseudonym 'Calliope'. It is for his talent in this direction that we have to thank him today when we read the poem he first published in 1794 entitled *A Poetical Description of the New South-End*.

It is a miracle that we are able to read it, for only two copies of it have survived. One of those was acquired for Southend Library through the foresight of J. G. Drysdale, a member of the library committee who had spotted it for sale in a bookseller's catalogue in 1936. This poem, 304 lines of clever rhyming couplets, shows us the state of Southend at the very outset of its development. It begins:

'GODDESS of song! that erst inspir'd the lays
Of tuneful Bards recording Baia's praise;
And thou sweet Nymph of Health, Hygeia, lend
Thy welcome aid to celebrate SOUTH-END.'

It goes on to show how the south end of the old village of Prittlewell is on the change:

'South of the village, but within its bound,
The recent fabricks proudly rise around:
In pleasant aspect by the river's side,
Where the steep cliff o'erhangs the foaming tide.'

Thomas Archer devotes quite a few lines to the hotels and inns even then springing up to meet the anticipated demand:

'Here the new buildings uniformly plann'd,
With southern aspect regularly stand.
Dispos'd with neatness, symmetry and taste,
In happy site and order aptly plac'd.
The grand hotel attracts an earnest gaze;
Whose front a column'd portico displays.
The public rooms well furnish'd and complete,
In size extensive, in arrangement neat,
Built on a large and elevated scale,
Of gen'ral approbation cannot fail.

The hosts at decent inns provide with care
Convenient lodgings and salubrious fare.
A spacious av'nue meets the London road;
Where splendidly in pompous portrait show'd,
York's beauteous Duchess, and the Royal Tar,
Invite the Traveller to stop his car,
Or soon (if more retir'd he wish to rest)
A private house accommodates the guest.'

The poet could hardly have been more prophetic when he used the word 'car' – though he was only shortening 'carriage' to suit his line. He goes on:

'Here with prophetic view the Bard descries,
Streets shall extend, and lofty domes arise,
Till NEW SOUTH-END in each spectator's eye,
With Weymouth, Margate, or Brighthelmstone vie.'

We should be very grateful to this man for giving us such a delightful picture of Southend in the days of its development from an ugly duckling as the outer edge of Prittlewell to the swan it is as a commercial, shopping, entertainment and holiday centre today.

Southminster

➤ This is a strange place of old and new. Estates have sprouted off a main street which is itself having to alter to cater for the growing population. The Memorial Hall, opened in 1933, performs all the functions of a civic centre, including nursery and library – at different times! It is a bustling place, but there is a phrase in the Essex guide of 1887 – 'It has a Reading Room, a Coffee Tavern, and Gas Works' which shows Southminster was already an urban if not to say urbane place of residence 100 years ago. Today the railway takes people to their London connections and commuters are prepared to arrive home late for the pleasures of living way out in the Essex countryside, halfway between the estuaries of the Blackwater and the Crouch. Due east there is just one lane which peters out in the Dengie marshes, still a wonderfully wild place where tracks and paths lead on to the sea wall and splendid views out across the North sea.

Opposite the Memorial Hall the church of St. Leonard has the most untidy-looking architecture of any church in the county. Even Nikolaus Pevsner calls it odd and aesthetically unsatisfactory. But forget the building, some of the furniture in the vestry is very interesting – a chart table, a bureau, a mirror, even the fireplace, were all once the personal property of Admiral Lord Nelson. They are here because Dr. Alexander Scott, who was appointed vicar of Southminster in 1806 had sailed away with Nelson on his conquering campaigns as his chaplain and his secretary. He it was who comforted the great man in his dying on the *Victory*, and when the ship came back to port he took these bits and pieces with him as personal, sad reminders.

Change is exemplified in the rise and fall of the Railway Hotel. A busy place when it opened in 1902, specially built in pleasing Edwardian style, it was in later years no more than a public house with a declining trade. London dealers no longer came to the famous Southminster Horse Fair and stayed the night. It closed in January 1988 and its goings-on have passed into folklore.

South Woodham Ferrers

Marsh Farm country park is part of this new small town created by Essex County Council in answer to the demand for more homes and workplaces in the south east. The government lent the council £8,000,000 to get the project off the ground. Standing in the town square, with all the buildings ranged about like grown-up versions of sets of Lott's building bricks, it is hard to imagine that 50 years ago there was nothing to be seen here but little farmsteads and smallholdings sinking into dereliction and despair as the depression bit deeper.

The bright new town remembers that agricultural past in Marsh Farm with its belt of farmland adjoining the river Crouch. It is a working farm with an information centre. Both are open to the public all the year round with animals at all stages of development, from lamb to ram. There is a place to picnic under cover, so there is no need to worry about the weather.

South Woodham Ferrers Town Centre

Very few of the inhabitants of the new town know that the old parish of Woodham Ferrers had a holy thorn tree, which, being of the same species as that from which Christ's crown of thorns was made, blooms every year on the day of his birth, Christmas Day. But we have to remember that, because eleven days were taken from our calendar in 1752 to make it agree with astronomical time, our Christmas is that much earlier and the thorn now blooms on 5th January. It was on that day in 1893 that the *Standard*, of London, reported that the Woodham thorn had burst into leaf on the stroke of midnight.

The rector, the Reverend Plumtree said, 'This tree is visited by more or fewer persons each year on the eve of January 5th. I have inquired of neighbours on the spot, and they tell me it produces buds and green shoots in the depth of winter. Indeed a credible witness informed me that he had gathered on that night this year a sprig with a small show of green on it. Even small May blossoms have appeared at this season in some years . . '

He did not say where the thorn tree grew, except that it was in a hedgerow in a somewhat distant part of the parish. Its roots are probably rotting under the bricks and concrete of that new town!

Springfield

━ Springfield Place, just up the hill from Chelmsford, was requisitioned during the Second World War to serve as a hostel for girls working at Hoffmanns, the ball-bearing manufacturers. One night two of the girls sleeping on the top floor awoke with fright; they said that something weird and horrible had touched their faces – then other girls spoke up about their experiences. Inquiries showed that years ago Springfield Place had the reputation of being haunted by the spirit of a man which wandered in the very rooms where the girls were sleeping. The warden solved the problem, calmed the girls, by putting new locks on the doors – so the papers say!

But looking further back in the history of the old house we

find that in 1868 Mary Petre, member of the celebrated Essex family, was woken up in the night by her baby daughter, feverish with teething. She took her into another room to save her husband being disturbed and laid on the bed with her. She must have dozed off for she was woken with a start by the baby's chuckle as it called, 'Funny man, funny man'. She looked up and saw a hideous, mis-shapen dwarf of a man standing by the fireplace. Mary wanted to hide under the bedclothes, but fear for her baby made her jump out of bed and confront the dreadful apparition. In that very moment it disappeared from her sight, though the baby still called, 'Funny man!' with apparent delight. Perhaps he had come, ugly as he was, to give that baby some relief in its fever.

It is only 25 years ago that a Springfield man swore he saw, one dark night, a woman in white walk out of the priest's door in All Saints' church and glide across to Springfield Place.

Stanford Rivers

➤ There are not many places which have the Lord of the Manor ready to research and write their history. Harold M. Scott did just this for Stanford Rivers in 1974 and made a very readable job of it. He gives such snippets of information as would slip through the net of a dry historian. For example, in October 1817 the villagers were so plagued by sparrows that the churchwardens offered 4d for every dozen of dead sparrows brought to them and 2d a dozen for their eggs. As to the look of the place he says: 'Here we find a very scattered population, divided into two distinct areas and residents must go to the nearest towns for the main shopping requirements and entertainments ... the passing motorist sees little of interest and is naturally quite unaware of the many interesting features revealed by my story of its past.'

Such features include the village fair which was held annually on 1st June on Sharpe's Green – Stewart's Cross today. The Cricket Club was active more than 100 years ago.

In 1904 it had a healthy balance in hand of £1 5s 9d. St. Margaret's church is described in detail from its founding around 1150 to the bell turret and spire added in the 15th century and the west porch built in 1812. In 1944 the whole south side of the church felt the blast of a German flying bomb. It was all carefully repaired, then in 1974 workmen on the bell tower and spire had some sort of accident and the whole thing was gutted by fire and once again restoration was required.

The Congregational chapel started in a cottage on the main road at Little End, moved to a purpose built chapel in 1820 and saw David Livingstone, then a student missionary at Chipping Ongar, step up to the pulpit to preach the sermon. He gave out the text, was totally overcome by stage fright, blurted out, 'Friends, I have forgotten all I had to say', and stepped down again. How we all know the feeling! Sad to say, the place which saw the very human side of that great man was burned down in 1927 through the upsetting of an oil lamp in a fire which also destroyed a Bible that had been Livingstone's personal possession.

On the main road one can see the most unusual use ever made of an old workhouse. It is a flag and tent factory established in the former Ongar Union Workhouse by Messrs Piggott in 1927.

Stansted Mountfitchet

What a grand name for such a small place – too much of a mouthful for modern advertising executives – the airport which has made this place famous round the world is simply called Stansted. Though that airport has bought up acres more land, demolished old houses or had them rebuilt elsewhere, it does not impinge to any great extent on the life of the small town two miles to the west on the other side of the M11. The nearest building to that road is the old parish church of St. Mary, with a most impressive brick tower built in 1662. In the north chapel there is a tomb chest with an effigy of a knight in armour. It was probably carved in the late 12th or early 13th century and may well be the resting place of Richard Mountfitchet, of the family which was rewarded by the Conqueror with 48 Essex manors.

They made their headquarters here and built a castle north west of the church on a spot between where the railway and the B1051 now run. Soon after Richard died the line failed and the castle began to crumble, only its keep was made of stone. There was practically nothing left of it until, recently, a new man bought the land, saw the potential public interest in such an old site and set about restoring it. The Norman motte and bailey castle has been 'replicated', the village which sheltered under its mound has been imaginatively reconstructed, and as the guide says, visitors can see a 'Complete living village and Castle'. Old breeds of animals have been introduced. There is no doubt that it all adds up to a great day out in the summer.

Then there is the windmill in the town, well to the west, which advertises itself with its strong, tall brick tower. It is open on certain days through the summer, giving visitors a chance to see the internal workings of a mill built in 1787 which worked until 1910 and was put back into working condition by the second Lord Blyth and presented to the town in 1934. Fifty years later another big restoration was under way which will allow both cap and sails to turn once again. From the money they have paid to keep their mill in order it is clear that the townspeople are very proud of their windmill.

Stebbing

➤ A church all built of stone in our stoneless county is a rare sight. Small wonder then that visitors head for St. Mary's. It looks the perfect parish church with its spire above its embattled, buttressed tower and its two rows of windows which flood the place with light pouring through their delicate tracery. The building is all of a piece, put up in the 14th century, though those buttresses show how it has been carefully maintained since then. The feature really to be enjoyed within is the very unusual rood screen stretching across the chancel arch. It is delicately carved in patterns too complicated to describe, and all in stone. There is only one other stone rood screen like it in the whole county, and that is at Great Bardfield.

There is another place, not of worship, but of work which any visitor should go to see, down on the Stebbing brook. As Hervey Benham says in *Some Essex Watermills*, '. . . in this village the town mill is among the most valuable survivals of all. Here, away on its own, down the lane beside the White Hart Inn, is a fine example of an 18th century corn mill, standing on one of Stebbing's two Domesday sites'. The beautiful white-painted clapboard mill, made all of timber under its tiled roof and jutting lucam, contrasts with the green of the trees which have grown up about it, beside the brook which adds another dimension to the picture.

It was being worked by miller Robert Dixon in 1823, Joseph Dixon followed him for 20 years then the Choppings took it on until 1882. From that year Henry Ruffel, one of the family which once made coaches in this village, took over and employed a young man who had already started there in 1863. His sons followed him and were able to buy the mill in 1931. Len Hynds, grandson of that young man, went into the mill as a school leaver in 1945 and became the owner and miller in 1959. Ken Ellis, local historian, tells us, 'In about 1905 flour production ceased and the mill went over to animal feed production only. The mill ran as a pure water-mill until the early 1960s when gradually electric power crept in until now only a pair of stones can be driven by the water wheel. However, on a few days in the year one can still smell the scent of freshly ground warm meal and hear the slap – slap – slap of the water wheel.'

Steeple

➤ Architects tend to sneer at the church of St. Lawrence and All Saints. It is a rebuilding in 1884, and on a new site, to the design of Frederick Chancellor, the Chelmsford-based architect. He used much of the material from the demolition of the old church, but mixed it up higgedly-piggedly with a brown stone and bricks in such a way that it looks, to the untutored eye, absolutely charming, the sort of village church that expatriates have in mind when they dream of home.

Old and new houses are mixed haphazardly on the village street. This dichotomy is well illustrated by the story of the public house, the Sun and Anchor. It was built in 1940, probably the only such house to have been erected at that difficult time, simply because it was already under way. Very modern at that time, it looked in stark contrast to the old public house which still stands next door, but has been divided into two handsome cottages named Sun and Anchor respectively. They formed the Anchor, built in the 18th century and reported in 1764 as having its weights and measures properly according to statute. For more than 30 years the Spurgin family ran it. Susannah Spooner and her son Summerset were running what was then called the Sun and Anchor. Christopher Whipps and his wife Ellen were the tenants of Grays, the Chelmsford brewers for 40 years from 1899, then their son Azel and his wife Victoria May took over and moved into the new Sun and Anchor.

Just one pub in a small village, but what a lot of life it has seen. The parish boundary to the north is the river Blackwater. A couple of narrow roads take the motorist on up to glorious views out down the estuary where the big power station is seen as a purple smudge on the horizon. But do not think you will be alone, walking the sea wall in glorious solitude; one road gives on to a holiday home and caravan park as well as the Steeple Sailing Club headquarters, while the other gives access not only to the vestigial remains of Stansgate Priory but also to the very lively premises of the Marconi Sailing Club.

Stock

➤ On the highest land in the village, the site of the present Roman Catholic cemetery, there is faint evidence of a rampart and ditch defence system. One local expert at least has dared to suggest that it could have been a stronghold of Queen Boadicea! He is on firmer ground when it comes to

Roman occupation, for remains of their pottery have been found in that same meadow, back in 1885. It was the Saxons who settled the place sufficiently to give it an identity and a name, which was written down in the register of property transactions called the Feet of Fines as 'Herwardstoc'. An interpretation of this one word might be that the steward of the local lord held this land which had so recently been cleared of the forest that the tree stumps, or stocks, were still there to be grubbed out.

The church was their skyscraper. The Saxons built it first, then, still using timber from the forest it was rebuilt some 700 years ago – a miracle of construction can still be seen today in the way in which the four great posts of the belfry were set up, braced and strutted to take the weight of the bells under the tall slim spire. A land mine fell in the churchyard during the Second World War, but that construction held. The windows were blown in and the walls were badly damaged, but all has been restored. The shattered gravestones were collected and, in 1953, were laid as a plinth to a memorial cross set up to mark the death of George VI. A circle of flowers grows all around and an engraved stone describes the circumstances.

In the church one memorial stands out. It is a brass to Richard Twedye who died in 1574, showing him in full armour. He was a brave soldier and a local benefactor as the inscription shows:

'Bewrapte in clay and so reserved until the Joyefull dome
Whoe in his lyffe hath served well against the Ingleshe foes
In fforen landes and eke at home his countrye well yt knowes
The prince he served in courte full longe, a pensioner fitt in personage
In his countrye a Justice eke, a man full grave and sage
Ffoure almeshowses here hath he builte for foure poore knights to dwell
And then indowed with stipend lardge enoughe to kepe them well . . .'

Those four almshouses, restored and modernised can still be seen on the little green opposite the church. In the process of modernisation a remarkable discovery was made. Under the floor of one cottage were found three large pots, buried before the hearth in a kind of circle with their necks touching in the middle. There is an air of mystery about it, and since these pots were made around the time that a woman in Stock was declared to be a witch, the strange position of these pots does send just a shiver of the supernatural. The witch, Agnes Sawen, tried in 1576, had a year in prison at Colchester and was made to stand in the pillory in the market place for six hours every quarter, subject to public humiliation while she confessed to her supposed sin.

Terling

This must surely be one of the most unspoilt villages in the county. Much of the credit must go to the Strutt family, elevated to the peerage as Lord Rayleigh since 1836, for the excellent, sympathetic management of their property. Its name comes from the river Ter which flows through the parish. On our visit we were told to pronounce Terling like darling. This is a place to walk about. To the west Gamble's Green is overlooked by the windmill, now a family home. Few people realise that it was originally designed not to produce flour but to grind bark, and that was in 1818. It was later converted to corn grinding and was run by the Bonners, father and son. The old man aged 78 was on his own in the mill on 30th March 1950 when he became entangled in the cogs. His screams were heard by his son, but he died before he could be freed. This was the tragic end of the story of the working windmill in Essex. The horrible coincidence is that this was the mill which had been used in the comedy film, *Oh! Mr. Porter!* starring Will Hay when a man was whirled round on the sails. By 1974 the conversion to a home was complete.

The wide ford across the Ter as we approach the centre of the village has been the undoing of more than one over-confident motorist putting his car at it like a horse at a water jump. Then there is a pleasant journey past any number of beautifully kept old cottages and colour-washed houses as one makes for the church of All Saints. Among many other interesting features look for the unusual sundial high up on the red-brick tower of 1723.

Terling Place, home of the Strutts is a beautiful late Georgian house, the centre part designed by John Johnson, the man who built Chelmsford's Shire Hall. Sometimes its gardens are open to the public in aid of charity – an opportunity not to be missed.

Thaxted

➤ When you stand in the beautiful church, enjoying the peace of the place, it is hard to imagine the cursing and swearing, the struggling and fighting which went on right in this church on Friday, 24th September 1647. The trouble was that, as Puritanism swept the country at the onset of the Civil War, the vicar of Thaxted, Mr Newman Leader, was replaced by a Mr. Hall. But Lady Maynard, who had the power to appoint the vicar would not agree. She wanted Edmund Croxon, even though everybody said he was a drunken blackguard.

She would not budge, so a great crowd of Thaxted people escorted their man to church and had him preach the sermon. When they tried to repeat the performance in the afternoon church officials barred their way. They were furious; they grabbed those officials, beat them up, tore out their hair in handfuls, made them flee for their lives. But the townspeople lost the day; their ringleaders were rounded up and taken for trial before the House of Lords that very same day, which shows how important the government and the church thought this sign of unrest in Essex was. A London bookseller jumped at the chance of a quick profit, selling a pamphlet hurriedly put together on 'The Great Fight in the Church at Thaxted'.

Believe it or not, that scene was re-enacted in the same church in 1921. This time it was the red flag which caused all the commotion. Lady Warwick, a Maynard before marriage, had chosen Conrad Noel as vicar. She was a committed socialist and he, grandson of the Earl of Gainsborough, was secretary of the Church Socialist League, so he had her full support. The trouble was that he went a bit too far in mixing communism with Christianity. High in the church, along-side the national flag of St. George he hung not only the flag of Sinn Fein but also the red flag of communism.

Cambridge undergraduates got to hear of it, came down to Thaxted in a body, borrowed a ladder, tore down Noel's flags and put up the Union Jack. Noel's supporters ripped it down, burned it, and replaced their flags. The shouting and swearing which it engendered was repeated yet again on Empire Day of that year when one of Noel's followers had his hat knocked off for failing to remove it when the national anthem was played. The fighting spilled out into the streets and cars and motor bikes had their tyres slashed. Were they really the Good Old Days?

Thorpe-le-Soken

➤ A hundred years ago the history book tells us, 'Thorpe is a neat little town; and its police-station, its magisterial meetings, and its small corn market, held on Wednesday evening, give it the dignity of the capital of the district.' Another 50 years before that it was the setting for one of the most romantic stories to come out of Essex.

Kitty was born in 1720 to Robert Canham, a well-to-do farmer who lived in Beaumont Hall, to the east of Tendring. She grew up happily and made a good marriage with the Reverend Alexander Gough, vicar of this parish. Her parents were so pleased and proud of their new connection with the church. It was not long, though, before Kitty was disillusioned with the humdrum of life in the vicarage. One day she just upped and left. She left not a word for her husband, changed her name so that she could not be traced and headed for London and the high life it offered.

By the sheerest good luck she fell into good company and was introduced to Lord Dalmeny, son of the second Earl of Rosebery. He fell deeply in love with her and asked her to marry him. She just could not tell her guilty secret. She married him, and their honeymoon stretched on and on. For four years they wandered round Europe. Then, at Verona, Kitty became ill. When she realised that death was inevitable she scrawled a note which read, 'I am the wife of the Reverend Alexander Gough, vicar of Thorpe-le-Soken in Essex . . . My last request is to be buried at Thorpe'.

That was in 1752, and amazing though it may seem, his Lordship carried out her wish to the letter, had her body embalmed, packed it in a special case and set sail for England. At the graveside the two husbands stood side by side, united in their undying love for one woman – little, pretty Kitty Canham.

There is still a rumour in this village that Sir William Gull, learned physician who attended the Prince of Wales and brought him through typhoid in 1871 was not buried in this churchyard as he should have been. His coffin was lowered into the grave, weighted with stones. He was himself not dead at all, but locked away in a private madhouse, because he was Jack the Ripper! Without digging up his coffin and opening it we shall never know.

Tilty

➤ The abbey here started by seven Cistercian monks in 1153 grew to buildings in stone, with a church built by 1221. By then a large community was tending vast flocks of sheep from which Tilty wool was harvested and exported throughout Europe because it was so fine. Then the hand of God moved in a mysterious way. The Black Death broke out in the abbey and so many brothers died that there were not enough survivors to run the large establishment, let alone expand it as they had hoped. It suffered the final indignity when it was closed by Henry VIII and its lands passed into secular hands. By 1542 Thomas Audley of Walden, the Lord Chancellor, had acquired the abbey. He tore it down to put up his own palace. In time that itself crumbled away and was gradually carted off for other purposes.

The only part of the abbey left was the chapel at the gate,

which the monks had allowed the villagers to use as their parish church. That use was allowed to continue, the church was repaired through all this time and stands today. The huge beautiful east window, with its delicate tracery is quite out of proportion with the present building; it shows how much more splendid the abbey buildings must have been. The church was open when we visited it and we were able to see the glass case with a wide selection of finds, curious and archaeological which have turned up on the site of the abbey in the meadow below the church, where one last wall remains.

It is unusual to be able to report that the tower was saved by tobacco. During the war, when tobacco was scarce the vicar, Hugh Cuthbertson, said in his parish magazine that he would pass on his secrets of successful tobacco curing to anybody who would pay five shillings towards the restoration of Tilty tower. A daily paper spotted this, let it be known nationally and Hugh received sacks of letters enclosing the necessary fee. So we may frown on tobacco today, but it did preserve that tower for us to enjoy and generations after us.

Tollesbury

So much to see down by Woodrolfe creek; the old fishermen's lofts, now restored and put to new uses, the well-organised marina, the footpath which will take you down to the estuary where the 'Crab and Winkle' railway made its last stop on the quay where it loaded up supplies for the famous jam-factory at Tiptree. But let us first stop by the church of St. Mary in the centre of this large village.

The feature which must surely catch your eye is the font, a pretty little octagonal bowl upon a graceful stem. Upon it a message is inscribed in gothic letters: 'Good people all I pray take care, that in ye church you do not sware, As this man did'. A puzzling message which, fortunately, can be understood by reference to the church's register of baptisms, now kept in the Essex Record Office, under the 30th of August 1718:

Fishermen's Sheds at Tollesbury

'Elizabeth, daughter of Robert and Eliza Wood, being ye first childe whom was baptised in the New Font which was bought out of five pounds paid by John Norman, who some months before came into the church and cursed and talked loud in the time of Divine service, to prevent his being prosecuted for which he paid by agreement the above said five pounds. Note that the wise rhymes on the font were put there by the sole order of Robert Joyce then churchwarden.'

If he had been put in the care of the constable he would have been locked up in the village 'cage' or lock-up which, restored and repaired in recent years, can still be seen in the corner of the churchyard.

Tolleshunt D'Arcy

What an attractive little village; with so many points of interest. Few such places have the good fortune to be described lovingly by a famous author for the benefit of future generations. Margery Allingham has done just that for Tolleshunt D'Arcy. She is famous for all those detective stories from *Flowers for the Judge* in 1936 to *Tiger in the Smoke* in 1952 which have been revived recently in a television series.

Born in London, it was after her marriage to Philip Young-man Carter that she came to live in this village. The house they chose to live in, Georgian-fronted D'Arcy House had been the home of the equally famous Doctor Salter. Margery's husband went off to war and she was left to make her own life in her new home. She soon got involved in village affairs and carried on writing. An American friend asked her to put down what the daily life of country people in England was like during the Second World War. So she wrote *The Oaken Heart*, all about her time then in Tolleshunt D'Arcy, though she actually called it Auburn.

There must be many an inhabitant today who remembers the old 'Crab and Winkle' railway from Kelvedon to Tolles-bury which she described:

'It is a nice little train with a high-pitched tootle and a fearsome tendency to rock like a boat in the high winds from over the saltings . . .'

Dr. Salter, born in 1841, took up the local practice in 1864 when, as he says in his diary he was, 'Received with great cheering at the entrance to the village'. His popularity went on increasing. He loved his patients and they loved him. He was a robust character, liked dogs and horses and even went to Russia to judge their dog shows. He is now remembered for his diary which included so much of the life of the locality. The original is now lost, possibly through the bomb-ing of Chelmsford in the Second World War, but a shortened version was printed and is in most of the larger Essex libraries. He died in 1932 and was buried beside his beloved wife who pre-deceased him by a year. His tombstone can still be read in the extension of the village churchyard.

He told of the fights the fishermen used to have with the Tolleshunt D'Arcy landlubbers outside the Queen's Head 100 years ago. Bert Sampson the landlord showed us how he keeps the public bar exactly as it looked in the 1920s, with furnishings all of a piece, from wooden wall benches and painted panelling to old-fashioned central heating cunningly camouflaged and from odd chairs, including a genuine 'Essex' example, to the flagged floor. Old prints of fishermen add to the nostalgia which makes the bar popular today with the fishermen and boating enthusiasts from Tollesbury.

The Pump and Puddingstone at Ugley

Ugley

➤ Every Women's Institute has its place-name before it – that is, every one except this village. After all, who would want to join an Ugley Women's Institute? So, by special dispensation it is called the Women's Institute of Ugley. It is a pity that the Old English name for the settlement, 'Ucga's little nook', has been so unfairly translated in modern times. It reminds us that the Saxon leader, Ucga, brought his family clan across the North Sea to start a new life in this verdant land where they cut down the forest and put up their hall and their church – focal points of their daily lives. Those sites are still occupied today by the later rebuildings of Ugley Hall and St. Peter's church, under the limes which dwarf the old brick tower of 1550. The church has to be kept locked because the centre of the village, down at Ugley Green is too far away for watch to be kept against vandalism.

Wander the churchyard and read the tombstone to the Jordan boys, Walter and Harry, who went away from Ugley's rustic tranquillity to the First World War – and did not come back. How grateful we are for the freedom they defended. Ugley has changed little since then, though there is a development of what you might call 'town houses in the country' in Patmore Fields just down the lane and round the corner. There is a pleasant but demanding walk down the rough bridleway to Ugley Green a mile and a half away. The car driver has to go down to the old A11, now the B1383 and turn off east. He or she will pass by Orford House built by Admiral Russell just after he was made Earl of Orford around 1700.

It has recently been bought by the Home Farm Trust, beautifully restored and adapted to meet the needs of young handicapped people who are thus enabled to live on their own, look after themselves and at the same time enjoy the company of friends. At the Green itself, the village pump still stands. Beside it is a great boulder of pudding-stone which was, no doubt, a signpost for prehistoric man, marking the track through the forest up the hill. Modern man rushes by on the M11 just a step to the east. He does not know what he is missing!

Ulting

➤ Ulting is not a particularly picturesque village. It does not gather round its church because All Saints stands in what can only be called a field rather than a churchyard, running down the hill to the very bank of the Chelmer. It is the only church right on the bank throughout the course of that river. Its attractions are its diminutive size, its 13th century architecture and its setting in such a lush, over-grown, riverside meadow. Sad to say it is its very isolation which requires it to be kept locked against vandalism.

There may be many Essex folk who have not heard of Ulting, yet it has a very important place in the story of Essex. It is the site of the first sugar factory in Britain. Part of the river Chelmer in this parish is still called 'Sugar Baker's Holes'. The sugar was extracted from sugar beet, a process invented by a German in 1747. Napoleon developed it to beat the British blockade of cane-sugar from the West Indies. By 1816 the French had set up 213 factories. It was not until 1832 that Britain became interested, when our Essex firm of Marriage, Reid and Marriage set up a sugar mill. It was sited right by the river so that vast supplies of sugar beet could be brought in by barge.

Their enterprise was strangled by a drop in the price of cane sugar. The mill closed and was eventually demolished, but that was not the end of the story of sugar in Essex. A big new factory, using modern methods was established at Felsted in 1926. Then the wheel of fortune turned again. National eating habits veered away from sweet obesity, much less sugar was consumed and so, in recent times that factory has also closed.

Waltham Abbey

➤ A precious document, written more than 800 years ago and kept in the British Museum tells the strange story of the building of Waltham Abbey somewhere around 1030. A blacksmith at Montacute in Somerset was told in a dream to get the priest and the villagers to dig a great hole in the hill above the village and they would find treasure. They dug, and they found deep in the ground, a huge stone cleft in two; inside it was an image of Christ on the cross all carved out in black flint. The local lord and landowner, Tovi le Prude, just knew that this was a sign from God. He hoisted the cross on to a waggon and harnessed to it twelve red oxen and twelve white cows. He said they would go wherever God willed, and prayed for guidance. He mentioned one holy place of pilgrimage after another, from Glastonbury to Winchester, but the animals would not move.

Then he thought of the little settlement in the woods in Essex called Waltham, where he was, at that time, having a country house built. He said its name – and the waggon moved as if it was directing the animals rather than the other way round. All those miles the waggon rolled, stopping while men and animals were refreshed, then pressing on remorselessly until it did come to Waltham and stopped for the last time.

The cross was tenderly lifted from the waggon and erected. Even as it was consecrated the great crowd that had gathered and followed it for miles saw blood flow symbolically from that flint image of Christ. Tovi was so overcome by it all that he gave his entire wealth to the founding of communities of the Holy Cross in Waltham, Kelvedon, Loughton and Alverton, which is probably the Alderton Hall of today.

Eventually ownership of the land passed into the hands of Earl Harold and the building of a magnificent church was put in hand. What the visitor will see there today is the rebuilding of 1242, with later additions.

Walton-on-the-Naze

'Miles of clean, sandy beaches – ideal for paddling, bathing and building sandcastles; exciting cliffs with acres of grassy play area at their summit . . .' – the district guide is absolutely right; these are the features our family has enjoyed over the years. There is more to it than that. For instance, the very long pier takes us out into the North Sea where we can look back and ponder on the reason for the tower which pokes up high almost due north. The answer is that the tower has no other purpose than to act as a landmark, put up on the Naze by Trinity House back in 1720. It guided shipping to the busy port of Harwich, and many a smuggler was grateful for it, silhouetted against the night sky, as he made for Hamford Water and the creeks that led far inland with his cargo of contraband, as described in *Smuggling in East Anglia*.

The real old village of Walton is now some nine miles out to sea, on the West Rocks. Its church finally fell into the sea in 1798. The new town grew from the early 19th century fad for sea bathing as a way to good health. Marine Parade was the first street completed, called then The Crescent. Now Walton has a very good shopping centre and all the amusements and recreation delights associated with the seaside.

It has more, in that the Naze is a marvellous, wild, grass-covered open space on the cliff which can swallow up crowds of people and still provide peaceful walks and picnics for family groups. Where the sea has eroded the cliffs below the Naze there is a particular geological deposit of earth known as the Red Crag; in it fossils of all kinds can be found from the sharks' teeth to the whale's ear bone shown in the Chelmsford and Essex Museum as the result of an outing to Walton many years ago. Looking for fossils is a favourite family pastime.

Wethersfield

➤ This is a huge parish, with hamlets like Beasley Green and Rotten End showing ancient houses with what must appear to Americans as careless abandon. There are plenty of Americans to photograph them with admiration for the Wethersfield air base is still operating. It was constructed by the Americans in record time in the winter of 1943–4 and their bombers flew their first sortie on 3rd March. Now it is manned by the 819th Civil Engineering Squadron, Heavy Repair of the United States Air Force. Their best landmark when they come to touch down is the tower of the church of

St. Mary Magdalen and St. Mary the Virgin, which was put up in the 13th century.

Tour the village, take in the 'wealth of old timbers' on display, visit the church, restored in 1874, then go on down via the narrowest of lanes to Great Codham Hall, which seems, on a quiet summer Sunday afternoon to be dozing in the 1920s, though the sight of modern machinery in the sheds and barns soon bursts that bubble of nostalgia. This is the last outpost of the parish, three miles from the church, overlooking the vale of the Pant, or Blackwater as some people will have it. The old Hall was just one room reaching right up to the rafters when it was built in the 14th century. In Tudor times it was divided into two storeys and into individual rooms. After that wings were added to increase the accommodation and then, in the 18th century the owner added the latest status symbol – an impressive facade.

Various important people have come to stay. One of them was Samuel Butler (1622–1680) who, while he was here, wrote part of his long, witty poem *Hudibras*, described by a Victorian critic as, 'Though sparkling with wit . . . is probably seldom read through. It is also defaced by many indecent and filthy passages'. Butler scratched his name on one of the windows, but that memento was too fragile – it broke.

Codham Mill, below the Hall, stopped work in 1956 after the Ashbys, father and son had been there for over 50 years. They checked the quality of their flour by using it themselves in a batter pudding once a week.

Witham

➤ When Witham's bypass opened on 15th September 1964 the town could breathe again, shoppers could actually cross the road. Since then the place has been expanded with London overspill people finding homes on the new estates and jobs in the new industries which have taken up sites reaching right out to the bypass. Exactly the same kind of town planning had been applied to Witham some 700 years ago, when the Knights Templar, with headquarters at Cress-ing, owned the land here. Then the town centre was Chipping Hill – a 'cheaping' was a market – but the Knights saw the advantages of setting up trade on the rapidly developing highway down by the bridge across the river Brain. Folk called it the New Land when gossiping about it in the market, and Newland Street it is still called today.

Between those ancient and modern developments there was yet another scheme of expansion, promoted in 1737. Dr. Taverner rediscovered a chalybeate spring just outside Witham. He aimed to make it the centre of a spa, with Witham becoming a second Tunbridge Wells. To this end he wrote a prospectus and had it circulated. Owners of properties all down the main street had new frontages put on to their shops, inns and businesses to impress the promised flood of customers.

The spa, however, did not take off; Witham metaphorically shrugged its shoulders and settled back again as a small market town and shopping centre. And that is what it is today, a pleasant place to drive out to and do one's weekly shopping – just for a change. Trade never returned to Chipping Hill, though there is still a blacksmith at work in the old forge – a craft centre if ever there was one. Nearby is the parish church of St. Nicholas. Roman bricks in its masonry prove the age of the settlement here. Inside there are two lovely surprises. One is the 15th century carved wooden rood screen with the cross still in position, which certainly must have been an oversight by the Puritan reformers of the Commonwealth period. The other is the altar tomb on which life-size effigies of John Southcote, a judge of the Queen's bench who died in 1585, and his wife are shown in their best dress in full colour – a wonderful evocation of 16th century costume.

Woodham Mortimer

➤ This is a place which motorists rush through on their way to Maldon from the west, forgetting that one of the world's most useful inventions was conceived here and kept secret for 100 years – the forceps used to help in cases of

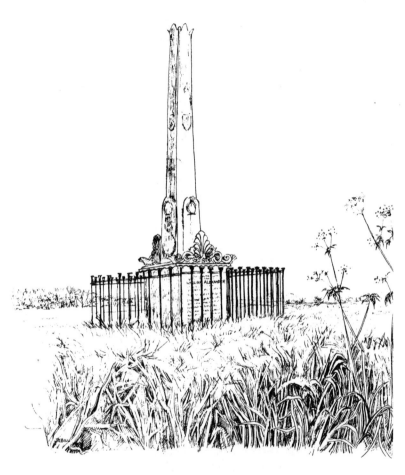

The Alexander Obelisk at Woodham Mortimer

difficult childbirth. It came about like this:

Peter Chamberlen, born in 1601, was a doctor, a 'man-midwife' as he was then called, of some importance. He followed his uncle as Physician Extraordinary to Charles the First and the Second. He kept out of the turmoil of the Civil War by buying Woodham Mortimer Hall, out in the country, but still within a day's ride of his practice in London. Here he brought up a family of 18 children. His great success with the royal and noble was due to his use of the forceps he had invented. He delivered children safely where, before, lingering labour had often led to the death of mother and baby. He would not allow other people into the room to see the way he worked. For 100 years succeeding generations of Chamberlen doctors achieved fame and fortune by the deft use of these forceps, until, early in the 18th century, an impecunious Chamberlen sold the secret to a Dutch surgeon who had them made for sale to the profession. In 1813, when the owner of the Hall was having a clear-out, a hidey-hole was found under a loose floorboard, and there, in a wooden box, they found Peter Chamberlen's original forceps! His body lies in the north east corner of the churchyard under a table tomb lavish in information yet ending,

'To tell his Learning and his Life to men:
Enough is said by here lyes Chamberlen.'

In the field on the other side of the road from the church a little square of railing protects an obelisk on which is written, 'In grateful remembrance of the munificent bequest by William Alexander Esqr. of his estate at Woodham Mortimer in the County of Essex for the benefit, behoof and advantage of the poor of the Company of Coopers, London, for ever, the master, wardens and court of assistants of the company have erected this memorial not only as a tribute of their respect and admiration but also with a view of publickly handing down to future ages so splendid an act of disinterested generosity, 1825.'

William Alexander, son of a publican, was born around 1673. Apprenticed to a cooper, he served a seven-year term until, in 1697 he was admitted to the Company as a fully-fledged cooper and set up his own business. He did so well that he was able to buy Woodham Mortimer Hall in its 300 acres of land and lease it out to a farmer. After his death the Company used the income to increase the pensions of retired coopers. In modern times the Company found they could get a better income from other investments so, in 1943, they sold the Hall farm to the sitting tenant, Stanley Ratcliffe.

Writtle

➤ The College of Agriculture stands on the site of a hunting lodge built for King John in 1211. It makes no fuss about this, after all there are so many points of historical interest in this village that justice cannot be done to them all in a short space. The most interesting book written about Writtle never went into print, but there is a copy kept in the Chelmsford library.

It was compiled by young students backed by Toc H and C.P.R.E. They came in July 1965 and camped out on the village green, and they went round asking questions and writing like fury. They found the Roman bricks in the church walls and went on to William the Conqueror taking over the Lordship of Writtle from the ousted Harold. They traced the connection of Robert the Bruce with the village and showed how Writtle was granted by Queen Mary to the Petre family of Ingatestone who is the present landowner today.

They inspected the two village greens, the three pleasant pubs and the fine parish church and they lighted on the entrance at the far end of St. John's Green, to what was then the research establishment of Marconi's, the wireless engineers and manufacturers. It was from this corner of the world that the first public wireless transmission of a programme was sent out to a marvelling public on 14th February 1922.

The College of Agriculture, Writtle

Index